UNLEASHING THE COLLECTIVE PHANTOMS

UNLEASHING THE COLLECTIVE PHANTOMS

ESSAYS IN REVERSE IMAGINEERING

BRIAN HOLMES

AUTONOMEDIA

*This book is dedicated
to the artists who dreamed it up between them,
and to the activists who wrote it out in the streets*

Layout & Design: Jim Fleming & Stevphen Shukaitis
Cover Design: Brian Holmes & Haduhi Szukis
The cover image is by Eva and Franco Mattes
aka 0100101110101101.org, from their project "Nikeground,"
carried out with Public Netbase in Vienna in 2003
(http://nikeground.com). Product names, logos, brands, and other
trademarks featured or referred to within this book are the property
of their respective trademark holders. These trademark holders are
not affiliated with Autonomedia in any way. We do not sponsor
or endorse these corporations or their products.

This publication is made possible in part
with funds from the New York State
Council on the Arts, a state agency.

Anticopyright @ 2008 Autonomedia & Brian Holmes
This book may be freely pirated and quoted for non-commercial purposes.
The author and publisher, however, would like to be so informed
at the address below.

Autonomedia
PO Box 568 Williamsburgh Station
Brooklyn, NY 11211-0568 USA

Website: www.autonomedia.org
E-mail: info@autonomedia.org

Printed in Canada

TABLE OF CONTENTS

01. Cartography of Excess   7
02. Unleashing the Collective Phantoms   15
03. Drifting through the Grid   29
04. Warhol in the Rising Sun   37
05. Maps for the Outside   37
06. The Revenge of the Concept   55
07. Liar's Poker   81
08. Policy of Truth   95
09. Artistic Autonomy and the Communication Society   99
10. A Rising Tide of Contradiction   115
11. Signals, Statistics & Social Experiments   121
12. S–77CCR   131
13. Three Proposals for a Real Democracy   137
14. Emancipation   147
15. Reverse Imagineering   157
16. Transparency & Exodus   175

1

CARTOGRAPHY OF EXCESS

BUREAU D'ÉTUDES & MULTIPLICITY

Utopian ideas—like "Spaceship Earth"—are round, multidimensional, interrelated: their archetypal map is the Milky Way, the infinite constellations. But rational thinking is instrumental, linear, it distorts: and that's exactly the problem with the Mercator map, the most common world projection. Buckminster Fuller, inventor of the geodesic dome, created a "Dymaxion map" to undo those distortions. First the earth becomes a geometric figure, an isocahedron: its twenty triangles are then disjointed and laid flat, so the land masses radiate from a nexus in the north, without splitting the continents or enlarging the polar regions. Fuller based his politics on this map: at the '67 World Expo in Montreal, in the dome of the U.S. pavilion, he wanted to lay out a vast Dymaxion projection and animate it with the most up-to-date statistics, so visitors could watch the flow of resources across the earth—and identify the structural patterns, the inequalities, the most wasteful or efficient solutions. Delegations from different regions would meet for cooperative sessions, in a problem-solving process called the "World Peace Game."[1] The idea behind it was simple: functional equality, radical democracy. "Make the world work, for 100% of humanity, in the shortest possible time, through spontaneous cooperation, without ecological offense or the disadvantage of anyone."[2]

Gerardus Mercator was a Protestant scholar from Flanders; he published his map in 1569, to help European merchants plot routes to distant shores. The ability to sail in straight lines led to the capitalist world-economy. Oyvind Fahlström was a Swedish artist who spent his childhood in Brazil, and died in the U.S.A. His *World Map* was painted in 1972, not long after Fuller imagined his utopia. Fahlström's map recalls the Mercator projection: but the oceans have practically vanished, the continents are crushed or swollen by the political pressures that the world-economy brings. Space overflows with clashes between the wealthy and the downtrodden, the CIA and the freedom-fighters, the capitalists, the communists, the revolutionaries. Fahlström was interested in resistance and excess: by which I mean politics plus overflowing subjectivity, statistics plus figurative invention. For him, a map was a flat, rule-governed space for a social game; but it was also an open territory for imaginary play.[3] In the early seventies he created a series of Monopoly boards (*CIA Monopoly*, *World Trade Monopoly*, *Indochina*, etc.), where political and economic information provides inflexible rules, whatever our passion, whatever our creativity. Yet a work like his *Pentagon Puzzle*—including a detail of a square earth, wrapped in chains—could also be taken apart, dispersed, its pieces reinserted into another game.

Fuller's utopia was not accepted for the U.S. pavilion in 1967: at the entryway, officials placed a huge golden eagle. But today, Internet access has brought tremendous quantities of information within our reach. Now everyone can play at mapping resources. "The communications aspect of my work can be vastly augmented by the use of computers and by the use of television, video and the miniaturizing trend of cassettes of video communication.... millions of people and multi-billions of dollars are at work in developing just such equipment, personnel and know-how," wrote Fuller in 1970.[4] Part of

Bucky's heritage is "osEarth Inc.," a think-tank and database compiler which organizes World Game sessions on a huge Dymaxion map, as a learning experience for youth. However, that experience is also sold to negotiating teams from Fortune 500 corporations. "Global civil society," with all its complicities and manipulations, is squarely on the map of our present situation.

Does anyone doubt that Fahlström's Monopoly paintings, with their focus on political confrontation, come much closer to the games the world really plays? Yet the recent round of counter-summits and global demonstrations still recall Fuller's basic ideas, functional equality, radical democracy. And one begins to wonder: where are the artist-cartographers of today?

POWER LINES

The Paris-based conceptual group, Bureau d'Ètudes, works intensively in two dimensions. For a recent exhibition called "Planet of the Apes" they have created integrated wall charts of the ownership ties between transnational organizations: a synoptic view of the world monetary game. Against a black ground, shield-like forms are emblazoned with the names of states, regulatory bodies, think tanks, financial firms and corporations. Texts on privatization and flexibilization are posted among the circuit-like arrays. A few spots give way to blue zones, humorous and surreal, like word-balloons or psychic oceans: these hold counter-information from autonomous groups, manifestos, constitutions, calls to action...

Instead of a catalogue, the visitor gets three "Wartime Chronicles," single sheets that divide the power players into overlapping regions. One is a finance pole, with pension funds, portfolio managers and banks, plus gray zones of legitimating foundations. Another shows media groups, networks of consumer distribution. So you want to call the police on these criminals? Military institutions, intelligence agencies, weapon makers and satellite companies complete the picture. A few quotes run along the sides of the sheets, like this one from the artist Fabrice Hybert: "My first collector, well, big collector... was a mediator for NATO and the big structures like that, NATO and the African or South American countries, something like that, another one is a mediator for all the arms industries, well, you know, it's horrible but he has this capacity to abstract himself in that scene... Me, I like people like that."5

If artists are talking in those terms, where can you escape? There's a wager in this exhibition: paint a totalitarian picture, totally black, and people will look for cracks leading into some other dimension. Another giveaway, the eight-page text called "Potentials," explores "autonomous knowledge/power"—or the deconstruction and reconstruction of complex machines—with a political analysis of different anarchist positions, as well as maps or figures listing dissident knowledge producers, squats and hacklabs, and a chart that relates various forms of non-capitalist exchange. A non-price (0 euros) and a contractual note figures on each of the sheets: "The present publication cannot be acquired, sold or destroyed. All persons may nonetheless use it as long as they please, with an obligation to give it to others if no longer desired." This last detail has its importance.

As Bruce Sterling put it: "Information Wants To Be Worthless"—worthless in monetary terms, that is.6 And far beyond the computer logic of free software, the great alternative project of the last decade has been mapping the transnational space invested primarily by the corporations, and distributing that knowledge for free. This is the real power of "spontaneous cooperation," in a global information project like Indymedia. Across a decade and more, from the early '80s to the mid-90s, the rules of the neoliberal economy were hidden in the back holes of offshore operations. Today, a multitude of projects like "Planet of the Apes" are making them increasingly visible.7 To the point where a new resistance means that we can start imagining—or exploring—a radically different map of the planet again.

Fuller would have loved the design of the Internet, which makes information-sharing possible for the World Game. Fahlström, the admirer of cartoonist Robert Crumb, would have loved the crowd at the Days of Global Action: autonomous and wild, intelligent and quick on their feet. Bureau d'Ètudes is in that crowd. By collaborating with squats, jobless people and *sans papiers*, by operating a self-organizing space in Strasbourg, the "Syndicat Potentiel," and combining it with "Université Tangente," a project for autonomous knowledge production, they have quietly begun transmitting a pragmatic intransigence to others on the French art scene, dominated by the likes of Fabrice Hybert. A new level of engagement was marked by their meeting with the No-Border Network for the Strasbourg camp in summer of 2002, an attempt to subvert one of the strongest power-lines: the Schengen Information System. Activities like those simply can't appear on the walls of the art world. In this sense, half the work of Bureau d'Ètudes remains underground: the refusals and denunciations are clear, the cooperation and subjective play remains almost invisible. And maybe it's better that way: how could you successfully *represent* an alternative, radically democratic experience?

UNCERTAIN USES

A sophisticated multimedia mapping project has tried to answer just that question. The screen before you shows a purple-black mass, spangled with mesmerizing constellations: slowly you realize it's a night-photo of urbanized Europe, with white rectangles marking zones of potential activity. The scene breaks: music plays, letters dance and roll, spelling out words; and you begin to wander within a matrix of slightly elevated, freestanding screens. You find yourself surrounded by distinct sets of imposing, static black-and-white images of architectural arrays; then snapshot color pics of people mingling freely in a everyday scenes; then sustained interviews in black-and-white with huge talking heads; then lyrical video strolls through some personal warp in the urban territory. Stop in front of one screen, and a specific, localized story unfolds: architectural setting, actors, individual story, subjective path through the city. Until the scene breaks, the language rolls, the music plays, and the permutations begin differently again. On the fringes of the art world, a group of urbanists has created one of the most impressive systems of visual representation to appear in recent years: *USE*, or "Uncertain States of Europe," a project by Stefano Boeri and Multiplicity.

Multiplicity is a networked research team, exploring the European territory as it changes, in twenty-six different sites from Athens to Espoo, from Porto to Bucharest or Moscow. The basic premise is that borders are ungraspable, that architectural programs and urban limits are unstable—but everywhere, the subjective excess of "autopoetic innovations" creates recognizable patterns of change, at least for the observer who mingles with them. For Boeri, whose aim is to deconstruct an outdated urban planner's gaze, what we are seeing is "the triumph of the multitude": consistently mutating but thoroughly unpredictable patterns of self-organization, niching in built environments that have increasingly lost their predetermined function. Thus one of the sequences (keyword: *détournement*) recounts how the uses of the Chinese community have completely transformed the ideal program of a huge modern housing block in the 13th district of Paris. Another (keyword: *eruption*) deals with the careful organization of chaotic raves, "nomadic flames": "The paths of the millions of ravers and tribes that invade Europe's streets every weekend bring us ever further away from a precise, functional destination."[8]

The reference to the multitude in Boeri's text, and indeed, on the screens of *USE*, recalls the political thinking of Italian Autonomia, with their central theme of "exodus," or conscious withdrawal from modernist planning and salaried labor. Obviously it's a dilemma for the traditional urbanist, or for any politician wanting to exercise control: "Escaping this condition of powerlessness simply implies accepting the ungovernability of a great deal of the contemporary territory," writes Boeri. This in its turn would mean "learning to act in a context directed by different, highly variable subjects."[9] What I'd call a situation of radical democracy.

But the big question that remains is how to use an installation like *USE*, and how to use the operational model of a networked, collaborative research group like Multiplicity. The exhibition device itself, elaborated outside the gallery-magazine-museum system, is the best installation I've yet seen on interactive social process: with its extensive matrix of screens, it opens up a real-and-imaginary territory, a multidimensional, interrelated world of subjective freedoms. But to what extent is it effectively political? "To resist is not to be against, anymore, but to singularize," writes Suely Rolnik, reflecting on the changing meanings of artistic practice since the Great Refusal of the 1960s. "All and any acts of resistance are acts of creation and not acts of negation."[10]

Beautifully said—but I'm not certain. The great theoretical swing of the past three decades, from critical negation to use value and subversive affirmation, has left "progressive" practices wide open to every form of cooptation and complicity. Despite the autopoetic processes that an installation like USE so brilliantly lets us see, the entire planet—Spaceship Earth— is prey to a resurgence of repressive authority, within the perfectly legible game of the capitalist world-economy. Berlusconi's Italy, where the project has been shown, is hardly an exception: and yet it is also one of the laboratories for new forms of political mobilization. Can we imagine artistic representations of self-organizing processes, in open confrontation with the economic game? "Rules oppose and derail subjectivity, loosen the imprinted circuits of the individual," wrote Oyvind Fahlström. Only then does a deeper territory emerge, a more complex interplay. Power lines/radical democracy.

NOTES

1. "The common assumption of ultimate war by the major political powers of our planet brought about the development of World WAR Gaming Science by the great powers' respective military strategists. World War Gaming Science involved all terrestrial resources. My World PEACE Gaming Science changes the basic assumption of fundamental inadequacy of total life support and applies total capability toward the success of all humans." Buckminster Fuller, "Preamble and Memorandum to those interested in playing World Game," in *The World Game: Integrative Resource Planning Tool* (Carbondale, Ill.: Southern Illinois University, typescript, 1971), p. 2, available at: www.bfi.org/worlddesign/WG1_Title.pdf. Fuller is, of course, the coiner of the expression "Spaceship Earth."

2. Quoted in Medard Gabel, "Buckminster Fuller and the Game of the World," at www.bigpicturesmallworld.com/BFuller.html. Thanks to Hubert Salden for putting me on this track.

3. I use Suely Rolnik's distinction between "playing-the-game" and "just-playing," in "Oyvind Fahlström's Changing Maps," exhib. cat. *Oyvind Fahlström: Another Space for Painting*, MACBA, Barcelona, 2001.
4. Buckminster Fuller, "Preamble and Memorandum," op. cit., p. 6.
5. Interview on May 2, 1996, with Fabrice Hybert, artist representing France at the Venice Biennial, in Bureau d'Ètudes, *Chroniques de guerre* 2, brochure, February 2002.
6. Bruce Sterling, "Information Wants To Be Worthless," distributed free over Nettime, March 6, 2002, archive at http://www.nettime.org. Let me recall that one of the richest Nettime threads over the years has concerned "the high-tech gift economy."
7. Mark Lombardi's sketch diagrams and index cards on banking scandals, or the website "TheyRule" by Josh On and Futurefarmers (www.theyrule.net), are close to the recent projects by Bureau d'Ètudes. "TheyRule" introduces a DIY side to corporate tracking: users can build up diagrams of a single CEO's participation in interlocking corporate boards. However, neither project has the synoptic ambitions of Bureau d'Ètudes.
8. Paolo Vari, "USE.04 Raves," in exhib. cat. *Mutations*, arc en rêve centre d'architecture, Bordeaux, 2000.
9. Stefano Boeri, "Notes for a Research Program," in *Mutations*, op. cit.
10. Suely Rolnik, "Oyvind Fahlström's Changing Maps," op. cit.

2

UNLEASHING THE COLLECTIVE PHANTOMS

FLEXIBLE PERSONALITY, NETWORKED RESISTANCE

In the best of all capitalist worlds, the stock market is supposed to provide resources for industrial development, through a speculative game that pays off later in the "real economy." What about the Internet then? From 1995 to 2000, huge amounts of infrastructure were financed throughout the world; now the oversupply crisis is accounted a disaster. But history is cunning, and the result of the dotcom boom may have been to free up vast amounts of private credit for the development of a virtual public space, where people can confront the major corporations on their home turf—that is to say, in the realm of transnational exchanges. The speculators of the late twentieth century asked: "Is there any limit to the profit we can make off the Internet?" Those who work for the virtual economy, or who suffer its effects, are tempted by a wilder speculation: "Can we really build a networked resistance to corporate capitalism?"

While dissenting movements face up to the new "anti-terrorist" campaigns, that last question is more timely than ever. Among the answers that emerge will be changes in the law, and in the course of technological development.[1] But the primary responses are cultural and artistic. They have everything to do with subjective capacities for resistance. And resistance itself has a history, with many different ruses. Those are what I'll be looking at here, to answer what might turn out to be the most important question: "Can the virtual class escape the domination of the flexible personality?"

PARADIGM SHIFT

From Taylor and Ford to Stalin and De Gaulle, the major adversary of the radical Left in the twentieth century was rationalizing authority. Whether on the factory floor or in the military ranks that gave the orders, regimentation and the hierarchical pyramid were the archetypes of oppression. From the 1930s onward, authoritarianism developed in both the East and the West, with a logic that brought together war, work and bureaucracy. The first to analyze this situation were the Frankfurt School.

The originality of the Frankfurt School was to combine Marx and Freud, to explore the industrial economy's masochistic libido. But to do so was not just to go beyond the pleasure principle. What the Frankfurt School studied from the 1930s onward was a paradigm shift: a new form of political-economic command that stretched its social fingers deeply into the psyche. The liquidation of nineteenth-century bourgeois individualism and the emergence of a central-planning state, along with a totally mobilized factory society, were internalized on the subjective level by what they called *the authoritarian personality*. They understood this fascistic character structure as a "new anthropological type." Its traits were rigid conventionalism, submission, opposition to everything subjective, stereotypy, an exaggerated concern with sexual scandal, emphasis on power and the projection outside the self of unconscious impulses.[2]

The Frankfurt School writers pursued their analysis of authoritarian behavior in the 1940s and 50s, in the face of American state capitalism. Exiles in the land of freedom, they denounced a deepening enslavement to instrumental reason, particularly through the soft coercions of the culture industry. By the mid-1960s, critiques of the disciplinary society became widespread. We are familiar with the new forms of revolt that arose against the standardizing forces: everything from free speech campaigns and draft resistance to Reichean group-sex, Provo events, situationist drifting and LSD, what Marcuse described as outbreaks of mass surrealism. On a deeper level there was an assertion of subjectivity, of identity, of sexuality, the personal that is the political. A poetics of resistance spread through society and helped bring the decline of regimentation, welfare-state bureaucracies, mass-consumption models and factory discipline. But are we even aware how that transformation helped shape today's political-economic system?

The social order responded to the crisis of the 1960s and 70s, accepting selected elements of the old critique. A new paradigm gradually arose in the developed countries, with its specific production regime, consumer ideology and social control mechanisms, all integrated to a geopolitical order. For almost two decades this development remained largely unconscious, invisible, unnamable. During that time, vanguard movements were obsolete, intellectuals were useless, there was no alternative. Then the cracks started opening up everywhere. From the mid-1990s onwards, increasing numbers of people would realize that the New World Order is not just oppressive on its edges, in the so-called developing countries. It has created a new regime of flexible labor that exploits and alienates broad swathes of the population, even in the places that are supposed to be rich. And it is at the very heart of casual freelance culture, replete with its PCs, mobile phones and general nomadism, that the technology of control is continuously recreated. Winning the economic game today brings a high reward. You get to be the inventor of *the flexible personality*.

CULTURE / IDEOLOGY

New paradigms are adopted because they work. Only in retrospect can we see them becoming modes of control. Flexibility was an extremely positive idea, in California in the 1970s when the culture of microelectronics was invented. It was the polar opposite of the rigid 1950s: openness to others, embodied experience, self-expression, improvisation, refusal of hierarchies and discipline. Those were the utopian days of Bucky Fuller, Gregory Bateson and the *Whole Earth Catalog*: no-one would have dreamed that *An Ecology of Mind* could become a management tool. But the looser, more creative lifestyle did not just mean the emergence of a whole new range of products, useful for stimulating consumption. In California, and ultimately in much of the developed world, the new culture seemed to promise a way out of the social conflicts that had stalled the Fordist industrial regimes.

Consider the way things looked to the Trilateral Commission, in their 1975 report on *The Crisis of Democracy*.[3] Not only were Third World countries using the powers acquired through national liberation to demand higher prices for their resources, while the US lost its war in Indochina. Not only were the capital returns plunging, while wildcat strikes multiplied and the big ecological standoffs began. But worst of all, the huge postwar investments into socialized education, conceived to meet the knowledge needs of the techno-economy, were backfiring and producing resistance to capitalism and bureaucracy, alternative values, demands for further benefits and socializations. These new claims on the welfare state had to be added to the traditional demands of the working class; and then the crisis began. In the eyes of the elites, the Trilateral countries were becoming "ungovernable," there was an "excess of democracy"—in the infamous phrase of Samuel Huntington. The kind of systemic critique that the Frankfurt School had pioneered reached its height in the mid-1970s. From that point forth, the authoritarian system had to start learning from the enemy within.

The transformation took a decade. The golden age of neo-management began in the mid-1980s, while unionized workers were replaced with robots and unskilled labor was sought overseas. Corporate operations and financial flows expanded outside core nations, where regulation and redistribution were called excessive. The triple challenge for the managers was to keep tabs on a distant work force, to open up global marketing and distribution, and above all, to create a culture – or an ideology – that would make significant amounts of younger people want to run this new machine. The keyword of the age was "flexibiity."

The social system had to accept and divert the demands for autonomy, self-expression and meaning; it had to turn those very demands into a new mode of control. The French sociologists, Boltanski and Chiapello, have shown how dependent this process was on the cooptation of what they call "artistic critique," which demanded mobility, spontaneity, the reduction of hierarchy, in short, disalienation—at least for the "creatives."[4] The rigid hierarchical pyramid would therefore be replaced, whenever possible, by the more open social form of the network. But an important aspect of the solution was directly technological. The magical answer to the questions that faced the governing elites of the 1970s turned out to be a communications device, a language-and-image machine: the networked personal computer. For the critical theorists of the 1960s, IBM had been the instrument and symbol of a disciplinary bureaucracy. Now the computer was going to set you free.

Freedom has always been the great neoliberal watchword, from Hayek and the Chicago economists to the right-wing libertarians and the Cato Institute. In their theories, it is constantly identified with economic initiative. On the left, the economy had traditionally been seen as the opposite of art, just as the act of selling is the opposite of the spontaneous gift. But the aesthetic strategies of the "counter-culture"—difference and otherness, the rhizome, the proliferation of subjectivities—could be exalted and set to work in a semiotic economy, where what you sell are images and signs. Such an economy had been rendered possible by telematics. Networked interactivity promised to divert a whole new alchemy of cooperative production into the same kinds of global channels that were already working for the finance economy. Research and invention could happen directly within the circuits of production, distribution and control.

The laptop computer freed up individuals for physical and psychic mobility; it could also be used as an instrument of control over distant labor. It miniaturized access to the remaining bureaucracy, while opening private channels into entertainment, media and the realms of "fictitious" capital—the speculative economy that feeds off the dismantling of the public sphere. Best of all, it recoded every kind of cultural production as commodities, multimedia. Here was a mode of development that might solve or at least gloss over the full set of problems inherited from the 1960s, particularly the struggles around the welfare state. Small wonder that the governments and the corporations started actively promoting a myth of flexibility. The emerging "virtual class"—including cultural producers, digital artisans, prosumers, what are now called "immaterial laborers"—stumbled more or less blindly into it.

GUIDANCE SYSTEMS

How does the culture/ideology work? War is popular these days, so let's take the military point of view. The weapon of choice during the Cold War was the ICBM: a huge, never-used giant, endlessly deconstructed by the critiques of phallo-logo-centrism. The New World Order takes off with a smaller, more practical device: the cruise missile. This kind of weaponry gets constantly used, and not just on the battlefield. Since the heyday of Star Wars—both the Strategic Defense Initiative and the Lucas movie—the military-entertainment complex has become part of everyday experience.

"It seems that retailers will go to any length to capture customers," reads a 1997 article called "Star Wars turns on to Shoppers" (quoted by Sze Tsung Leong in *The Harvard Guide to Shopping*). "Witness Safeway, which has recently used an artificial intelligence system from IBM called AIDA (artificial intelligence data architecture)—which was initially developed to detect and identify Russian missiles in space, but is now used... to analyze information on buying patterns with details of purchase from loyalty cards." When consumer desire is "turned on" and encouraged to proliferate, the ultimate control fantasy becomes that of tracking the flexible personality.

"Mass marketing, for all intents and purposes, is dead," writes business guru Art Weinstein, in *Market Segmentation*. "Precision target marketing... has taken over. By focusing on ever smaller yet profitable market segments, stronger company-customer relationships transpire. With technological products, users can practically invent markets for companies—customers become customizers." When feedback devices are built directly into the distribution circuits, the sources of desire are directly available to corporate monitoring. Any new expression deemed useful for your seduction will be sent back to you in a commodified form. So you can help perfect your own internal guidance system.

Until recently, such trends seemed comfortably ambiguous—just the irritating price for increased freedoms. But with security-fever rising after September 11, everything starts to look different. The incitement to perform, to find creative ways of deploying the new equipment, reveals its hidden face, the fear of the excluded other, the imperative to ruthlessly extend and perfect the system. And the system really is threatened, not only by suicidal terrorism: the collapse of the "new economy," the growing protests against neoliberal globalization, the revolution against the IMF in Argentina... The perfect solution is total mobilization, the shift to a wartime footing. September 11 was a chance just waiting to be taken—the chance to consolidate the new paradigm, on every level.

The American artist Jordan Crandall has made the military compulsions of the networked system visible. His work began with the heritage of the 1970s: experimentation, cooperation, networked performance, adjustment to the presence of others in virtual space. But in 1998, he hired a freelance military contractor to help him develop movement-predicting software, whose algorithms show up as eerie green tracery around bodies in a video image. The following exhibitions, *Drive* and *Heat-Seeking*, were full-fledged explorations of the psychosexual relations of seeing and being seen, through the new technologies in both their civilian and military uses.[5]

A text recently published on Nettime, "Fingering the Trigger," recounts the use by the CIA of an unmanned, camera-and-missile-equipped Predator drone to fire upon a suspicious Afghani man who, it turns out, was probably just scavenging for metal. "We align eye, viewfinder, and target in an act of aiming," Crandall writes. "But we are aimed at, we are constituted in other acts of looking. These are analysis and control systems in which the body is situated.... It sees us as a nexus of data, materiality, and behavior, and uses a language of tracking, profiling, identifying, positioning and targeting.... Within the circuitous visualization networks that arise, one never knows which 'side' one is truly on, as seer switches to that which is seen; as targeter switches to that which is targeted." Crandall thinks a new sexuality lodges in the body-machine-image complex; hence the image of the soldier-man "fingering the trigger."

This work helps us see what the easy money and pluralism of the Clintonian years kept hidden: the outlines of a social pathology. It has an authoritarian cast, like everything that involves the military. But it does not produce unthinking, stereotyped behavior, of the kind we associate with 1930s fascism (or today, with Le Pen). What Crandall describes is an extremely intelligent process that, precisely by individualizing—tracking, identifying, eliciting desire, channeling vision and expression—succeeds in binding the mobilized individual to a social whole. The new fascism discovers a complex, dynamic order for subjective difference, perspectival analysis, *jouissance*, even schizophrenic ecstasy. It integrates networked individualism.

GHOSTS IN THE MACHINE

Arthur Kroker had an inkling of these things. Over a decade ago, he and Weinstein wrote about the "liberal fascism" of the "virtual class": a technological elite, driven by possessive individualism, whose interests lay with the financial establishment, the military state and the big corporations. But like all neo-situationists in Baudrillard's wake, Kroker is obsessed by "the recline of the West" and the hypnotic power of the digitized image: "The virtual class is populated by would-be astronauts who never made it to the moon," reads a passage from *Data Trash*. "They do not easily accept criticism of this new Apollo project for the body telematic."

No doubt that was true, in 1994 when Kroker's text was written. But the massification of Internet access, pushed by the needs of globalized management, and hailed everywhere as a catalyst of technological development, has brought about the opening of the virtual domain to political critique, and to social movements. At the close of the millennium ordinary citizens began exploring transnational space, which had formerly been the sole preserve of the elites. One of major activist efforts since the late 1990s has been to map out the new modes of domination, in order to identify the planetary division of labor, beyond the spectacular flux of images (and of financial information). Another attempt, less accessible to the general public perhaps, but decisive for the struggles that became visible in 1999 in Seattle, has been to create a poetics of resistance: a *virtual class struggle*, alongside the embodied one that never disappeared.

Consider the AAA, founded in 1995 with a five-year mission: establishing a planetary network to end the monopoly of corporations, governments and the military over travel in space. The Association of Autonomous Astronauts is a kind of multiple name, a freely invented identity. Forget about the moon: "Reclaim the Stars" they said on June 18th, 1999, during the Carnival against Capital in the City of London. The idea was to create not an art group, but a social movement—a collective phantom acting on a global scale. "Unlike a multiple name that is restricted to art practices, a collective phantom operates within the wider context of popular culture, and is used as a tool for class war," says an astronaut of the South London AAA, in a text called "Resisting Zombie Culture."[6]

One aspect of the project was infrastructural mapping, identifying the satellite hardware that links up the world communications network. But another was what Konrad Becker calls "e-scape": "Cracking the doors of the future means mastering multidimensional maps to open new exits and ports in hyperspace; it requires passports allowing voyages beyond normative global reality toward parallel cultures and invisible nations; supply depots for nomads on the roads taken by the revolutionary practice of aimless flight." Ricardo Balli gives a further idea of what the galactic phantom might do: "We are not interested in going into space to be a vanguard of the coming revolution: the AAA means to institute a science fiction of the present that can above all be an instrument of conflictuality and radical antagonism."[7]

The ideas sound fantastic, but the stakes are real: imagining a political subject *within* the virtual class, and therefore, within the economy of cultural production and intellectual property that had paralyzed the poetics of resistance. Consider Luther Blissett, an obscure Jamaican football player traded from Britain to Italy, who fell short of stardom but became a proliferating signature, the "author" of a book called *Mind Invaders: Come fottere i media* (How to fuck the media). There, between tales of Ray Johnson and mail art, Blissett takes time out for some political-aesthetic theory: "I could just say the multiple name is a shield against the established power's attempt to identify and individualize the enemy, a weapon in the hands of what Marx ironically called 'the worst half' of society. In *Spartacus* by Stanley Kubrick, all the slaves defeated and captured by Crassus declare themselves to be Spartacus, like all the Zapatistas are Marcos and I am all we Luther Blissetts. But I won't just say that, because the collective name has a fundamental valence too, insofar as it aims to construct an open myth, elastic and redefinable in a network...."[8]

The "open myth" of Luther Blissett is a game with personal identity, like the three-cornered football played by the AAA: a way to change the social rules, so a group can start moving simultaneously in several directions. This "fundamental valence" lies at the prehistory of the counterglobalization movement. Just think of the way names like Ya Basta, Reclaim the Streets, or Kein Mensch ist Illegal have spread across the world's social networks. One can see these names, not as categories or identifiers, but as catalysts, departure points, like the white overalls (*tute bianche*) worn initially in north-eastern Italy: "The Tute Bianche are not a movement, they are an instrument conceived within a larger movement (the Social Centers) and placed at the disposal of a still larger movement (the global movement)," writes Wu Ming 1 in the French journal *Multitudes* (#7). This "instrument" was invented in 1994, when the Northern League mayor of Milan, Formentini, ordered the eviction of a squatted center and declared, "From now on, squatters will be nothing more than ghosts wandering about in the city!" But then the white ghosts showed up in droves at the next demonstration. And a new possibility for collective action emerged: "Everyone is free to wear a *tuta biancha*, as long as they respect the 'style,' even if they transform its modes of expression: pragmatic refusal of the violence/non-violence dichotomy; reference to *zapatismo*; break with the twentieth-century experience; embrace of the symbolic terrain of confrontation."

Yet a strange thing happened, explains Wu Ming in another text: "Some rhetorically opposed the white overall and the blue overall, and the former was used as a metaphor for post-Fordist labor—flexible, 'precarious,' temporary workers whom the bosses prevent from enjoying their rights and being represented by the unions."[9] Between politics, class uncertainty and sheer word play, the Tute Bianche got into full swing. The technique of "protected direct action"—allowing ludicrously padded protestors to face blows from the police—was a way to invade, not just the media screens, but above all the minds of hundreds of thousands of other people. They converged in Genoa in July 2001, to open a real political debate in a country stifled by a neofascist consensus.

Another example of the effects created by a confusion of identities are the Yes Men, in their cameo or "chameleo" appearances as representatives of the World Trade Organization. Here we're talking about two artists, whose names aren't hard to discover. But the uncertainty over language is no less interesting. To say "yes" to neoliberal ideology can be devastatingly satirical, as when the self-elected WTO representative "Hank Hardy Unruh" displayed the logical fiction of the *Employee Visualization Appendage*, a telematic worker-surveillance device in the shape of a yard-long golden phallus. No one has yet imagined a better caricature of the flexible personality. But what kind of satire is at work when Kein Mensch ist Illegal takes the neoliberal ideology seriously, and declares all the world's borders open, for everybody? Like the fire-colored masks worn by thousands at the FTAA summit in Quebec City, today's networked protests have two faces: the laughter of open communication, or the violence of a gagged mouth behind a chain-link fence. Both faces are the truth of the contemporary political confrontation.

VOICE AND EXIT

No doubt millions of the world's "flexible" workers remain largely gagged—mute—with no voice and no hope of escaping. But as use of the Internet has increased, and as people have seized its communicational power for both organization and subversion, a metamorphosis has invaded the "transnational public sphere," which formerly was only open to corporations and their governments. Electronic e-scape—a new form of the exit strategy, an exodus from the national space—has been a condition for the access to political voice, far from being its contrary.[10] It is in the Deleuzian sense that dissent became virtual in the late 1990s: virtuality as latency, as potential reality, flight-lines towards other spaces of creation and confrontation.

The virtual class in this sense, or the immaterial laborers—I've always preferred to say *networkers*—cannot *stand in* for the rest of the world's population. There is no universal subject to represent, when the individual, the supposed bearer of human rights, increasingly becomes a target for technological and ideological manipulations. But an active indistinction of identity has begun to spread, like a new departure point; and the artistic experience of multiple names reveals one of the possible paths toward a renewal of collective autonomy. In a recent text, the Italian philosopher Paolo Virno locates the universal in pre-individual aesthetic and linguistic experience, in the impersonality of perception and circulating language. The chaotic dissension of public space then becomes the landscape, not of defensive individualism, but of evolving paths to individuation: "Far from regressing, singularity is refined and reaches its peak in acting together, in the plurality of voices, in short, in the public sphere."[11]

The kinds of conflicts that began in the universities in the 1960s have crossed over into the global knowledge-space of the Internet, whose nature as a public domain in now intensely at issue. To what extent will these networks form a space of cooperation, and to what extent a space of intensified control? If new political voices confirm an exit from the flexible personality, and a refusal of liberal fascism, then there will have been no waste in the wild speculations of the late 1990s—whatever the multiple names of the investors.

Notes

1. On the closely intertwined relation between legal and technical aspects of the net, see Lawrence Lessig, "The Internet Under Siege," pdf at www.lessig.org/content/columns/foreignpolicy1.pdf.
2. Cf. Theodor Adorno et. al., *The Authoritarian Personality*, (New York: Harper, 1950). For more on the theories of authoritarianism and their dialectical reversal in our time, see my text "The Flexible

Personality," in *Hieroglyphs of the Future* (Zagreb: Arkein / WHW, 2003); available in author's archive at www.u-tangente.org.
3. The European rapporteur of *The Crisis of Democracy* was the French sociologist Michel Crozier, author of an important book entitled *La société bloquée* (*The Stalled Society*). The American rapporteur, Samuel Huntington, has not ceased to make his views known since then.
4. See Luc Boltanski et Eve Chiapello, *Le Nouvel esprit du capitalisme* (Paris: Gallimard, 1999).
5. For the work of Jordan Crandall, see his book *Drive: projects and writings 1992–2000* (Cantz Verlag/ZKM, 2002), as well as his website, http://jordancrandall.com.
6. Written under the name of Boris Karloff, at www.uncarved.org/turb/articles/karloff.html.
7. The two quotes are taken from a French anthology of the AAA, edited by Ewen Chardronnet: *Quitter la gravité* (Nîmes: L'éclat, 2001); online at www.lyber-eclat.net/lyber/aaa/quitter_la_gravite.html.
8. Luther Blissett, *Mind Invaders, Come fottere i media: manuale di guerriglia e sabotaggio culturale*, chap. 1, "Ray Johnson e Reggie Dunlop tra i Tamariani," at www.lutherblissett.net/archive/215_it.html (there is an English translation but it's incomplete and loose; and the Italian book it not the same as the one published by Stewart Home under the same title).
9. Wu Ming I, "Tute Bianche: The Practical Side of Myth Making," at www.wumingfoundation.com/english/giap/giapdigest11.html.
10. The opposition between the functions of "exit" and "voice" in social conflicts was theorized by Alfred O. Hirschman, in a book to which the Italian theorists of exodus frequently refer: *Exit, Voice, and Loyalty: Responses to Decline in Firms, Organizations, and States* (Cambridge, Mass.: Harvard University Press, 1970).
11. It is in this sense that the "multitudes" are still before us, emerging through exchanges and acts, unlike the prepolitical multitude described by Hobbes. Cf. Paolo Virno, "Multitudes et principe d'individuation," in *Multitudes* 7.

Esther Polak, *Amsterdam RealTime: A Diary in Traces*, 2002.

3

DRIFTING THROUGH THE GRID

PSYCHOGEOGRAPHY & IMPERIAL INFRASTRUCTURE

Great social movements leave the content of their critical politics behind, in the forms of a new dominion. This was the destiny of the revolt against bureaucratic rationalism in the 1960s. The Situationists, with the practice of the *dérive* and the program of unitary urbanism, aimed to subvert the functionalist grids of modernist urban planning. They sought to lose themselves in the labyrinth of a *Naked City*, while calling for the total fusion of artistic and scientific resources in "complete decors": "Another City for Another Life," as the radical architect Constant proclaimed.[1] With the worldwide implementation of a digital media architecture—and the early signs of a move toward cinematic buildings—we are now seeing the transformation of the urban framework into total decor (Lev Manovich: "In the longer term every object may become a screen connected to the Net, with the whole of built space becoming a set of display surfaces"[2]). What kind of life can be lived in the media architecture? And how to explain the continuing prestige of Situationist aesthetics, in a period which has changed so dramatically since the early 1960s?

Today, the sensory qualities of the *dérive* are mimicked by hyperlinked voyages through the datascapes of the World Wide Web. The comic-book imaginary of the Silver Surfer still permeates our computer-assisted fantasies. Within this commercialized flux, the proponents of "locative media"—like Ben Russel, the developer of headmap.org, or Marc Tuters, of gpster.net—propose to add a personalized sense of place, a computerized science of global ambiances, using satellite positioning technology. In this way, the "geograffiti" of GPS waypoint marking seeks to promote a new kind of locational humanism, tailored to the worldwide wanderer. "Know your place" is the ironic HeadMap motto. But what would it really take to *lose yourself* in the abstract spaces of global circulation?

Not long ago (during the speculative boom of the 1990s) the utopian maps of visionary engineers could portray the Internet as an organic space of interconnected neurons, like the synapses of a planetary mind. Data-sharing and open-source software production have effectively pointed a path to a cooperative economy. But a mapping project like *Minitasking*, elaborated in 2002, depicts the Gnutella file-sharing network as a seductive arcade, bubbling over with pirated pop tunes and porno clips. The revolutionary aspirations of the Situationist drift are hard to pinpoint on the new, hi-tech cartographies.

In the wake of September 11, the Internet's inventors—DARPA, the Defense Advanced Research Projects Agency—conceived a new objective: Total Information Awareness, a program to exploit every possible control function that can be grafted onto the new communications technology. Here's where the innovation lies: in "Evidence Extraction and Link Discovery," "Human ID at a Distance," "Translingual Information Detection," and so on. Fortunately for our civil liberties, the U.S. Congress still had the constitutional power to quash this distorted brainchild of a convicted political criminal, the retired admiral John Poindexter. But the Pentagon has clearly caught up to the commercial surveillance packages that took the initiative in the late 1990s: workstation monitors, radio-tracking badges, telephone service recording, remote vehicle monitoring (advertising blurb: "From the privacy of your own computer, you can now watch a vehicle's path LIVE using the new ProTrak GPS vehicle tracking device"). Military strategist Thomas Barnett has learned the lesson of those freewheeling years, when all across the world, individual autonomy developed at the speed of high technology—until Mohammed Atta finally found himself at the controls of a 767. "In my mind, we fight fire with fire," Barnett says. "If we live in a world increasingly populated by Super-Empowered Individuals, then we field an army of Super-Empowered Individuals."[3]

In "The Flexible Personality" I tried to show how networked culture emerged as a synthesis of two contradictory elements: a communicative opportunism, bringing labor and leisure together in a dream of disalienation that stretches back to the 1960s; and an underlying architecture of surveillance and control, made possible by the spread of cutting-edge technologies. The contemporary manager expresses the creativity and liberation of a nomadic lifestyle, while at the same time controlling flexible work teams for just-in-time production. The Yes Men have made this figure unforgettable: impersonating the WTO at a textile industry conference in Finland, they unveiled a tailor-made solution for monitoring a remote labor force, what they called the Management Leisure Suit. The glittering lycra garment might have recalled what *New York Times* pundit Thomas Friedman once called the golden straitjacket, forcing national governments into the adoption of a neoliberal policy mix; but the yard-long, hip-mounted phallus with its inset viewing screen is just a little too enthusiastic for private-sector discipline! Transmitting pleasurable sensations when everything is going well on the production floor, it allows the modern manager to survey distant employees while relaxing on a tropical beach. The conclusion of the whole satirical charade is that with today's technology, democracy is guaranteed by Darwinian principles: there's no reason for a cost-conscious businessman to own a slave in an expensive country like Finland, when you can have a free employee for much less, in whatever country you chose.[4]

What happens when the freedmen revolt? Today all eyes are on the soldier. Thomas Barnett has drawn up a new world map for the Pentagon: it divides the "functioning core" of globalization, "thick with network connectivity," from the non-integrating gap of the equatorial regions, "plagued by politically repressive regimes." The gap is where the majority of American military interventions have taken place since the end of the Cold War. It's also where most of the world's oil reserves are located. And it's mainly inhabited by indigenous peoples (in Latin America) or by Muslims (in North Africa, the Middle East, Central Asia, Indonesia). Barnett's solution: "Shrink the gap." Integrate those people, by force if necessary.

Jordan Crandall seems to grapple with this question of integration in one of his installations, "Heat Seeking." The piece is full of menacing violence; but one scene shows a passive, unconscious woman being fed, apparently under the influence of a radio transmission. This disturbing image gets under the skin of the new media architecture, exploring its relations to psychic intimacy.[5] What kind of subjectivity emerges from exposure to the contemporary networks?

I think we should conceive the worldwide communications technologies—such as the Internet and the Global Positioning System — as Imperial infrastructures. These are systems with strictly military origins, but which have been rapidly liberalized, so that broad sectors of civil society are integrated into their basic architecture. Everything depends on the liberalization. The strong argument of Hardt and Negri's *Empire* was to show that constitutional legitimacy is necessary for the spread of a reticular governance, whose inseparably military and economic power cannot simply be equated with its point of origin in the United States. Imperial dimension is gained when infrastructures become accessible to a new category of world citizens. The effect of legitimacy goes along with integration to the "thick connectivity" of which Barnett speaks.

What happens, for example, when a private individual buys a GPS device, made by any of dozens of manufacturers? You're connecting to the results of a rocket-launch campaign that has put a constellation of twenty-four satellites into orbit, at least four of which are constantly in your line-of-sight, broadcasting the radio signals that will allow your device to calculate its position. The satellites themselves are fine-tuned by US Air Force monitor stations installed on islands across the earth, on either side of the equator. Since Clinton lifted the encryption of GPS signals in the year 2000, the infrastructure has functioned as a global public service: its extraordinary precision (down to the centimeter with various correction systems) is now open to any user, except in those cases where unencrypted access is selectively denied (as in Iraq during the last war). With fixed data from the World Geodetic System—a planetary mapping program initiated by the US Department of Defense in 1984—you can locate your own nomadic trajectory on a three-dimensional Cartesian grid, at any time, and anywhere on Earth (Defense department dogma: "Modern maps, navigation systems and geodetic applications require a single, accessible, global, 3-dimensional reference frame. It is important for global operations and interoperability that DoD systems implement and operate as much as possible on WGS 84").

Perhaps the most interesting aspect of this satellite infrastructure is that in order for one's location to be pinpointed, the clock in each personal receiver has to be exactly synchronized with the atomic clocks in orbit. This is the first operation the system performs. So you have an integration to Imperial time. The computer-coded radio waves interpellate you in the sense of Althusser, they hail you with an electromagnetic "hey you!"[6] When you use the locating device you respond to the call: you are interpellated into Imperial ideology. The message is that integration equals security, as exemplified in the advertising for the Digital Angel, a personal locative device pitched to medical surveillance and senior care. It's a logical development for anyone who takes seriously the concept of the "surgical strike": give yourself over to the care of the nurturing machines, target yourself for safety.

In light of all this, one can wonder about the limits of the concept of conversion, developed extensively by Marko Peljhan in quite brilliant projects for the civilian reappropriation of military technology. Can we still make any distinction between a planetary civil society articulated by global infrastructure, and the military perspective that Crandall calls "armed vision"? The urgency is social subversion, psychic deconditioning, an aesthetics of dissident experience. These are the disruptive elements that constitute what Deleuze and Guattari call "the nomadic war machine."

Most of the alternative projects or artworks using the GPS system are premised on the idea that it permits an inscription of the individual's path, a geodetic tracery of subjective difference. The most beautiful example to date is Esther Polak's *RealTime* project, where GPS-equipped pedestrians gradually sketch out the city plan of Amsterdam, as a record of their everyday itineraries.[7] But the work is a fragile gesture, fraught with ambiguity: the individual's wavering life-line appears at once as testimony of human singularity in time, and as proof of infallible performance by the satellite mapping system. The beauty of the former can act to hide the latter's insidious potential.

All too often in contemporary society, aesthetics is politics as decor. Which is why the Situationists themselves soon abandoned Constant's elaborate representations of unitary urbanism. "Ideology represents the imaginary relationship of individuals to their real conditions of existence," wrote Althusser. It's what makes you walk the line, to use his image. Has the ideology of our time not become an erratic, wavering pattern of crisscrossing footsteps, traced in secure metric points on an abstract field? The aesthetic form of the *dérive* is everywhere. But so is the hyper-rationalist grid of Imperial infrastructure. And the questions of social subversion and psychic deconditioning are wide open, unanswered, seemingly lost to our minds, in an era when civil society has been integrated to the military architecture of digital media.

Notes

1. Text available at www.notbored.org/another-city.html.
2. See the text by Lev Manovich on "Augmented Space," downloadable at: www.manovich.net/DOCS/augmented_space.doc.
3. Thomas Barnett, *The Pentagon's New Map* (Putnam, 2004), as well as the article at www.thomaspmbarnett.com/published/pentagonsnewmap.htm.
4. For the story of the Finland lecture, see www.theyesmen.org /hijinks/tampere/index.shtml.
5. See documentation of this work at www.jordancrandall.com.
6. See Louis Althusser, "Ideological State Apparatuses," in *Lenin and Philosophy and Other Essays* (New York: Monthly Review Press, 2001), p. 119; a pirate version of this famous paper is available at www.culstudies.com/rendanews/displaynews.asp?id=2534.
7. See the documentation at http://realtime.waag.org.

Andy Warhol

4

WARHOL IN THE RISING SUN

ART, SUBCULTURES & SEMIOTIC PRODUCTION

In the wake of Andy Warhol, the artist-producer Takashi Murakami is looking for his quarter-hour of fame—or better, his quarter-century. Murakami is the creator of computer-assisted wallpaper works, but also the designer of manifesto-exhibitions, which claim to define a new Japanese art. The most recent of these, on display in summer 2002 at the Cartier Foundation in Paris, was called *Coloriage*, or "Coloring Book." Inspired by the mangas—a flagship product of the Japanese cultural industry—the exhibition brought together a short list of artists and a mind-boggling series of children's toys: mascot characters, action figures, animated films, Pokemon cards and comic books. Murakami's idea is that a veritable renaissance of Japanese culture is being asserted in these commercial works: "Today we create new outlines on our own—disordered perhaps, but ours, without any origin in the Western 'fine arts.' This new movement finds its origins in what the West calls subculture. *Coloring Book* is created by Japan, a country which does not distinguish between culture and subculture." In this way, he concludes, a "new *Japonisme*" is emerging.[1]

Also in Paris, the Palais de Tokyo—"site of contemporary creation"—wants to blur the distinction between art and commercial subcultures. Here, "the visual arts play the role of a *search engine* leading to design, cinema, literature and fashion."[2] Halfway between the art center and the nightclub, the Palace aspires to be a theater of lived events, where the visitor can seamlessly drift from the contemplation of objects—art, design, fashion, etc.—to experiences of use and participation. This is a legacy of "relational art," which posed the aesthetic object as a catalyst of subjective formations. The discourse of relational art functioned perfectly on the French scene of the 1990s. It acquired a touch of exoticism and a higher potential for distribution with the addition of the signifier "Tokyo," connoting nomadic lifestyles and the enigmas of meaning in a multicultural world, but also the automation of a high-tech society and the fascination of media products. The same signifier has been added to an entire series of projects: *Tokyo Games* (works for video consoles), *Tokyo TV* (artist's clips), *Tokyo Books* (art world opinion polls), *Tokyorama* ("alternative" tours through the museum's luxury neighborhood)... In this way the Palace seeks to develop into a hybrid workshop, where artists can try their hand at all the genres of semiotic production,[3] which they individualize and develop in a minor mode. But what results from such a transformation?

Takashi Murakami claims a double heritage from Warhol. On the one hand, as a painter-illustrator working with a team of assistants (about twenty) to produce canvases that are at once sophisticated and kitsch; but also, in a more complex way, as a promoter of fashions and trends, via events conflating art works, media glamour and commercial design. The Palais de Tokyo, as an institution, takes its place within the larger turn of contemporary art in the 1990s toward teamwork processes modeled on audiovisual production and interaction design, integrating the public's reception of the work.[4] In this way, using new tools and addressing a far wider public, the Palace seeks to functionalize Warhol's experimentation in the Factory, where the practice of film served to transform marginal subjectivities—members of the gay and lesbian subcultures, drug addicts, bohemians escaping their class origins—into "superstars," in a transgressive parody of the Hollywood system. The

Factory can be seen as a deliberate subversion, not only of the standardized model of the postwar culture industry, but literally of the mass-production system and its Fordist discipline. This subversion took the form of collective expression from below: the irruption of subterranean cultures into the normative frame of the cinema. But that was forty years ago. Today, Takashi Murakami gestures toward the same potential when he appeals to the creativity of a very different subcultural fringe: the *otaku*, those young Japanese who increasingly remain hooked on mangas and video games, even after the age of thirty when the passage to adulthood is supposed to be definitive. And the Palais de Tokyo also adopts this subcultural pose, disguising itself as an artificial squat, complete with graffiti, raw walls and (fake) disconnected plumbing, smack in the middle of the chic 16th arrondissement of Paris. What is the meaning of such postures today, in the postfordist era? And what exactly is a subculture, if it is no longer to be distinguished from the official, normative one?

To ask these questions is to open up a double analysis: both of semiotic production and of contemporary control (or biopower). But it is also to confront the enigma of the *otaku*: those playful creatures of pure consumption, who devote their adult lives to an artificial childhood, and pierce reality's bubble with their joysticks. Abandoning oneself excessively, but in a deliberately trivial way, to all the traps of the entertainment industry; risking one's adolescent revolt on a bid to become the perverse, but perfectly willing appendage of a product or an image: this would seem to be the dream of these Japanese youth, yanked off the standard track by their overstated allegiance to a dominant ideal.

MIRRORS OF RECEPTION

Since the introduction of the consumer society on the island in the decades after the Second World War, the Western gaze wants to see the "normal" Japanese citizen as totally passive, subjugated to the fascinations of fashion. The *otaku* then becomes the disquieting figure of this passivity.[5] In parallel, theories of active reception developed in the West. Since the emergence of British cultural studies, an entire scholarly literature has arisen to illustrate the possibilities of subjective development offered by the mass-produced product, when it is diverted by singular uses. Initially, the idea was to point out class differences in the reception of standardized messages. One of the most famous works in this vein, Dick Hebdige's *Subculture, or the Meaning of Style* (1979), analyzed the way that fashions in clothing and music could be used by proletarian and immigrant youth communities in London as identifiers in a play of semiotic differentiation, constantly evolving across the urban territory. While these "deviant" practices were packaged by major record labels for national and planetary audiences, Hebdige himself, caught up in the excitement of early punk, dreamt of a style that could dissolve into the air at will, escaping from the capture devices. But his dream of exodus would be oddly lacking in the great unfurling wave of reception studies that followed. With the passage to Australia, then to the United States in the eighties, these studies came increasingly to bear on identifications with the stars (Madonna, Travolta) or on the most banal consumption situations (hanging out in the local mall). From an adversarial subdiscipline, cultural studies became almost hegemonic: so that in Japan one can now aspire, in all seriousness, to the status of a majority subculture.

In the mid-nineties, Thomas Frank and Dave Mulcahey did a scathing parody of these theoretical trends, suggesting the uses they could unwittingly serve. The text takes the form of an article counseling the purchase of a particular stock, like those you find in the publications of the Bloomberg group (one of the sponsors of the Palais de Tokyo):

> Consolidated Deviance, Inc. ("ConDev") is unarguably the nation's leader, if not the sole force, in the fabrication, consultancy, licensing and merchandising of deviant subcultural practice. With its string of highly successful "Sub-Cults™," mass-marketed youth culture campaigns highlighting rapid stylistic turnover and heavy cross-media accessorization, ConDev has brought the allure of the marginalized to the consuming public.[6]

In a flash of wit, this text shows exactly how the functionalization of subcultural styles gives rise to a regime of semiotic production, inseparable from an Imperial mode of control. The music industry offers the clearest example. A musical style from a "problem neighborhood" is plucked from its context (anywhere in the expanding planetary ghetto), cleansed of its local dross (struggles too complex for a single chorus), recoded for transmission in a standardized medium (CD or video clip) and broadcast to the clientele of the global entertainment corporations (Sony, MTV, Virgin Megastore). Here is one of the mainsprings of the postfordist economy. The advantage of the process, in terms of control, is to break up the development of resistance groups on the local territories through a destabilizing injection of money, even while holding out a mirror of "recognition" to the bearers of an ephemeral subculture—a glittering mirror that becomes the object of desire for all those who haven't yet "broken through." Variations of style, even attempts to put together a counter-style (as in the territorial struggles described by Dick Hebdige), continuously serve as raw material for the functionalization of new products and images. Despite the occasional exceptions (bands like Zebda or the Asian Dub Foundation), this mechanism has proven extremely difficult to resist. And all that helps us to understand at least one of the meanings of a condition where culture is no longer distinguished from subculture: it is the now-hegemonic condition where minority styles and even individual forms of subjectivization are constantly surveilled, but constantly encouraged too, so that they can be brought into relation with mirror-products capable of stimulating their differences—before they are parasitically captured at the opportune moment, for functionalization and translation into economic profit. In this way Warhol's Factory, a vanguard experiment of the Fordist era, has become the model for the contemporary social factory, under the regime of semiotic production.

We are clearly very far from the hopes of the academic researchers who gathered around Stuart Hall in Birmingham in the early seventies, thinking that they could find a kind of gap, or even a possible space of emancipation, in the semiotic variations that emerged between the processes of broadcasting and reception (or, as they said, between the "encoding" and the "decoding" of media messages).[7] One could even suggest—but it's all too easy in retrospect—that the Birmingham researchers did not look closely enough at the ambiguity of Warhol's treatment of the subcultures converging at the Factory. Because there is no doubt that Warhol took a genuine interest in the subjectivity of his haphazard stars (Edie Sedgewick, Gerard Malanga, Mario Montez, the

Chelsea Girls...), with whom he carried out a process of collective experimentation, even while using photography, film and video to record the entire range of emotions and interactions that could arise between the participants. But at the same time, and with no less determination, he sought to appropriate Hollywood's means of production and distribution. In a perspicacious text, Juan Suarez remarks that Warhol's deepest desires for success were frustrated by the lack of access to the distribution machinery, and also by his actors' scanty fame. Only through the exploitation of his own status as a painter in the media glow, and more, as a kind of avant-garde impresario gifted in the eyes of his audience with an almost magical power to create, could he achieve the distribution he sought: "Through his ability to turn marginal performers into superstars, daily objects into art objects, and gestures and styles into media images, Warhol incarnates the absolute producer, able to make the most out of the least, to increase the value of whatever came into his orbit, no matter how banal or inconsequential."[8] Beneath the camera-eye of the absolute producer, an entire group of haphazard artists can attain their "fifteen minutes of fame"; but the producer himself will build a far more enduring legend. The directive powers accruing to this privileged role of the artist-producer—which Takashi Murakami, like so many others, seeks to fill today—is what the exponents of cultural studies did not take into account, when they located a subjective gap between the moments of encoding and decoding, of distribution and reception.

A JAPANESE TURN?

The ambiguity of the artist-producer is that of the *political entrepreneur*, theorized in the studies of immaterial labor.[9] A charismatic figure, but always dependent on his project team, the political entrepreneur works in creative fields such as fashion, music, or audiovisual production. He can choose to channel the collective activity of the team towards his own ends, in order to parasitically extract a monetary gain; or he can lead the project in such a way that the working collective develops its diverse capacities and finally dissolves, leaving behind a gain in competence and charisma for everyone. The same model applies to the artistic field. Thanks to the progress in miniaturization, carried out notably by Japanese engineers, we live in societies where the means of image production are within everyone's grasp: the artist's role becomes that of catalyst, of organizer. Positioning himself among the multitude of image makers, the artist-producer can orient his work to encourage subjective multiplicity; or he can invent capture-devices, playing on mirror-products and reception-effects. The "relational artists" whom one finds at the Palais de Tokyo (or at the Musée d'art moderne just next door) find themselves at grips, perhaps unwittingly, with exactly this choice between two outcomes. And curiously enough, it is through the diversion of a Japanese manga film that a group of these artists—circling around two "producers" —now offer us a kind of logical conclusion to the work of the Western theorists on the question of reception. They have created a collective portrait of the artist as otaku.

The project *No Ghost Just A Shell* began in 1999 when Pierre Huyghe and Philippe Parreno purchased the rights to a low-end manga character (few distinctive features, no pre-written biography). The title refers to an animated film, *Ghost in the Shell* (1996), the first "Japanimation" blockbuster to be released simultaneously in the US, Japan and Great Britain; it relates the tribulations of a female cyborg, Motoko Kusanagi, concerning the existence or non-existence of her soul. The game will then be one of breathing various artistic souls into the empty manga shell, which nonetheless receives a name, Annlee. Huyghe and Parreno launched the process with very simple animated films, where the former asserts that Annlee is a "deviant sign," and the latter, that she "belongs to all those who can fill her with whatever kind of imaginary materials." Some fifteen creators did so, replaying the well-known miracle of cultural studies, whereby the standardized product is individualized through its reception. The computer-graphic commodity opens its mouth, becomes a speaking being, endowed with multiple tongues. The artists' collective comes to form a kind of ephemeral subculture, identifying itself around the product that it transforms. And then the owners of the rights to the character orchestrate the transfer of these rights to a non-profit association, whose aim is to "withdraw" (or, they also say, to "liberate") Annlee from the domain of representation, by forbidding any ulterior use of her image. The existing sum of visual interpretations is brought together in an exhibition, the exhibition as a whole is sold to a Dutch museum, and the entire project is consigned to our reflection in form of a luxurious volume, published by the purchaser, the Van Abbemuseum, and signed by Huyghe and Parreno.[10] Their quarter-century of fame now appears certain.

And yet everything remains unthought here, concerning the status of majority subcultures and the functions of reception theory. We know that Warhol gave up the name of the Factory in the early eighties, remarking that we had shifted to the era of the "Office"—that is to say, of management. The decade was marked by the "monetary turn" of the American economy, and by the emergence within the financial sphere of what the economist Yoshihiko Ichida calls "the Imperial circuit," funneling Japanese capital to the USA.[11] The regime of semiotic production, which had emerged with the use of informational just-in-time techniques in Japanese factories, but also with the miniaturization of computers, now imposed itself in the West; there it gave rise to the new forms of flexible management, both of a highly mobile global workforce and of highly volatile financial instruments. The distance separating Japan from the European countries became more relative, as all the cultures (including America's) became the "subcultures" of Empire. And it was in this context that the analysis of reception—whose great ambition had been to transform the cultural hegemony by introducing "other" voices—itself became a management tool, in the service of a new hegemony. One of the great techniques of biopower, closely intertwined with semiotic production, would now consist in "making people talk" about commercial objects—somewhat the way that the disembodied intelligence of a futuristic secret agent, in the film *Ghost in the Shell*, seeks first to make the cyborg Motoko Kusanagi speak, then to occupy her body.

How to escape this paradigm? In the course of the nineties, movements of cultural rebellion began to constitute themselves in excess of any identifiable signature, through the playful exchange of multiple names, which became "collective phantoms" open for unlimited appropriation. Elsewhere I have described the subversive potential of this cultural trend, whose best-known avatar is the ubiquitous Luther Blissett.[12] These practices of collective dis-identification gesture toward broader fields of cultural experimentation, marking an exodus from the mercantile and bureaucratic system that imposes strict controls on the circulation and use of its knowledge-products.13 But the current development of the art world's institutional market, based on its own star system, leaves little room to explore such inventions in the museums. The signature of the artist still acts as a mechanism of closure, of copyright, as the now-completed story of Annlee seems to demonstrate. Only when artists finally abandon these closed spaces—overflowing their bounds through practices of unlimited circulation—will a new sun rise finally over the world of art, which the dark star of Warhol still dominates today.

Notes

1. See the exhibition descriptions at www.fondation.cartier.fr.
2. Quoted from the press package distributed for the opening of the institution.
3. The "linguistic turn" of postfordism has been described by C. Marazzi, in *La place des chaussettes*, l'Éclat, 1997; Italian edition 1994. For a succinct description of what I mean by a "regime of semiotic production" see Marcos Dantas, "L'information et le travail," in the anthology *Vers un capitalisme cognitif*, (Paris: L'Harmattan, 2001).
4. Pioneer, a Japanese manufacturer of audiovisual equipment and content, whose American subsidiary has commercialized the Gundam action figures presented in the Murakami exhibition, is among the sponsors of the Palais de Tokyo.
5. A typically sulphurous image is provided by E. Barral: *Otaku, les enfants du virtuel*, (Paris: Denoël, 1999).
6. T. Frank, *Commodify Your Dissent*, Norton, 1997.
7. S. Hall, "Encoding/Decoding" (1973), in *Culture, Media, Language*, Hutchinson, 1980.
8. "The Artist as Advertiser," in *Bike Boys, Drag Queens, Superstars*, (Bloomington: Indiana University Press, 1996), p. 246.
9. For the ambiguities of the political entrepreneur, see A. Corsani, M. Lazzarato, A. Negri, *Le Bassin de travail immatériel (BTI) dans la métropole parisien*, (Paris: L'Harmattan, 1996). A definition of the

artist-producer, with a central reference to Warhol, has been furnished for the French art world by Dan Graham in "L'artiste comme producteur" ("The Artist as Producer," 1988, in D. Graham, *Rock/music Textes*, (Dijon: Presses du réel, 1999).
10. *No Ghost Just A Shell*. (Cologne: Walther König, 2003).
11. See Yoshihiko Ichida, "Circuit monétaire impérial et capture financière de valeur," in *Multitudes* 13, Paris, Spring 2003.
12. See the text in this volume, "Unleashing the Collective Phantoms."
13. For a useful text on the cooperative production of informational and cultural goods, see Yochai Benkler, "Coase's Penguin, or Linux and the Nature of the Firm," available at www.benkler.org/ CoasesPenguin.html.

5

MAPS FOR THE OUTSIDE

"CONCEPTUALISM" IN THE WORK OF BUREAU D'ÉTUDES

The closure of the gallery space is a classic conceptual gesture. Witness this proposal by Robert Barry: "My exhibition at the Art & Project Gallery in Amsterdam in December, '69, will last two weeks. I asked them to lock the door and nail my announcement to it, reading: 'For the exhibition the gallery will be closed.'"[1] Conceptual art can be defined, not simply as the refusal of the commodified object and the specialized art system, but as an active signage pointing to the outside world, conceived as an expanded field for experimental practices of intimacy, expression and collaboration—indeed, for the transformation of social reality.[2]

Thirty-two years later, in October–December 2001, the French group Bureau d'Etudes reiterated the gesture, sealing off the exhibition space of Le Spot, a converted industrial building in the port city of Le Havre. Instead of a simple sign, they confronted the visitor with a book,

Juridic Park, which upon closer inspection proved to be a detailed set of maps to the "legal subsoil" of the city. But these maps, like the more recent cartographic projects, do not simply gesture to the outside of one of modernity's specialized subsystems (the feedback loop of gallery-magazine-museum). Instead, they detail the proliferating closures of a totally administered society, where almost every square inch of terrain is strictly codified for exclusive, proprietary uses.

The name of the group, "Bureau d'Etudes," denotes an expert consultancy, a study office for technical research. Theirs is an intensely precise apprehension of the world, shot through with flashes of dark humor. But their work in its broadest dimensions is also the foundation, or perhaps the springboard, for an antagonistic utopia.

BEGINNINGS

In 1998, with the exhibition *Archives du Capitalisme*, Bureau d'Etudes started producing organizational charts showing the proprietary relations between financial funds, government agencies, banks and industrial firms. A number of these graphic charts, or "organigrams," were deployed as part of an installation including black-and-white photographs of heads propped up on wooden pickets (presumably CEOs), as well as a scale model of a proposed new parliament building, to articulate the voting rights of those with real power in today's society. The exhibition was an autonomous project in an artist-run space, at the time called the "Faubourg," in the city of Strasbourg. For a subsequent show entitled *Le Capital*, mounted by Nicolas Bourriaud in the city of Sète, an organigram detailing the relations between the French state and a panoply of major transnational corporations was blown up to wall size. Squares and rectangles of varying proportions, each identified with a name—Société Générale, Dresdner Bank, Mitsubishi, Pirelli, etc.—were connected with a labyrinth of elaborately traced channels, printed in black against a white ground. The result was something like an all-over painting for the computer and finance-obsessed 1990s: an aesthetics of information. In other words, one of the historical failure-points of what has been called "conceptual art."

Sooner or later, artists working on the analysis and transformation of social reality must face the obvious question: How to escape the formats, publics and modes of exchange that are offered by the gallery-magazine-museum system? The answer is a gradual process, a social and psychic experiment. Invited to a group exhibition for which, as usual, they would not be paid, Bureau d'Etudes responded by creating a "zone de gratuité," *Free Land*, where treasures and all kinds of junk could be deposited and taken away without the intermediary of money. The experiment of the free zone was pursued in a gallery/living-space in Paris, where theoretical curiosity and the more practical prospect of something-for-nothing drew a variegated public. Expanding on the question of the artist's real social status in an age of casual labor and mass intellectuality, Bureau d'Etudes worked with Alejandra Riera, Andreas Fohr and Jorge Alyskewycz to launch the "Syndicat Potentiel" or "Potential Union," a proto-political association addressed to all the intellectual and cultural producers whose aspirations lead them outside the existing professional categories. The key ideas here came from the French anarchist traditions, but also from theories of the gift economy, developed by the anthropologist Marcel Mauss and reworked by French social critics after the great strikes of 1995, in an era of structural unemployment.[3] Among the first co-operators were the group Plus tôt te laat, from Brussels—jobless artists who had occupied an unemployment bureau, transforming it into a center of expression and reflection on the meanings of work in contemporary society. Such reflections in turn led to increasing proximity with the squatters' movements, whether in France, Italy or Germany. From these beginnings, Syndicat Potentiel grew into an open-ended frame for intimate and networked collaborations, with the explicit goal of producing autonomous counter-knowledge, oriented toward an economy of *gratuité totale* (in which basic services such as living space, water, electricity, access to communications media, etc. would be "totally free").[4] The project continues today, giving its name to the self-managed space in Strasbourg where the art group had produced its earliest proposals.

OPPORTUNITIES

It is against the almost invisible background of Potential Union and a parallel project, "Tangent University," that the recent cartographic projects deserve to be understood. They came as an unexpected, long-desired opportunity. The rupture of consensus brought by the Global Days of Action, beginning in May of 1998, served to galvanize the wider counter-globalization movement, through innovative uses of the Internet as a worldwide distribution system operated from below. A kind of autonomous, do-it-yourself conceptualism began to emerge, whereby "attitudes become forms": an idea or phrase arising in one locality (for instance, "Our Resistance is as Transnational as Capital") becomes a geographically distributed political performance (the "Global Street Parties" against the annual G8 reunions).[5] In perfect accord with Lawrence Weiner's famous dictums, the work could be carried out by the initial authors of the ideas, realized by others, or not done at all—something like a taste of planetary exchange, where the "art" is "totally free."

Even as these protest forces emerged on a large scale—mapping out the power structures of globalization with their feet, as it were—the rise of the information society and the deregulating thrust of neoliberalism had made it possible for relatively small, highly mobile groups to appropriate and to use advanced technologies, acting upon extremely sophisticated visions of the world. Yet these new possibilities for the application of specialized research were not immediately visible in France, due to language barriers, a pitifully conservative art scene, and critical discourses dominated by the aging communist professors of ATTAC. Perhaps it was as late as December 2001, with massive protests at the EU summit in nearby Brussels, that the potential for a more active distribution of the antagonistic maps became clear to Bureau d'Etudes. Further institutional projects, at La Box in the city of Bourges, then at Kunst-Werke in Berlin, served as occasions for the initial production of graphic charts in large print runs, for broad distribution. These helped prepare the knowledge and the skill-sets needed for two autonomous, collaborative productions, both printed in thousands of copies for specific activist events: *Refuse the Biopolice*, for the No Border Camp in Strasbourg in July 2002, and *European Norms of World-Production*, for the meetings of the European Social Forum in Florence in November of that same year.

This delayed access to the counter-globalization movements meant that the antagonist maps, with their extraordinary complexity of analysis, have come at the right time—after the initial breakthroughs of the first period of dissent met their enforced pacification and partial neutralization, as a consequence of the violence unleashed by the police riot in Genoa. Both these maps present an excess of information, shattering subjective certainties and demanding reflection, demanding a new gaze on the world that we really live in. These are synoptic visions of the contemporary, transnational version of state capitalism, as constructed "by collusion between specific individuals, transnational corporations, governments, interstate agencies and 'civil society' groups."[6] They make visible the elite institutions that have structured themselves in an overarching, terrifyingly abstract space, almost totally beyond the grasp of the democratic counter-powers formerly exercised within the purview of the national states, and indeed, almost totally invisible to localized populations—at least, until recently, when the new communicative possibilities have allowed a certain measure of "cognitive mapping" to be performed by inhabitants.[7]

Refuse the Biopolice, focused on contemporary control systems, also offers more detailed readings of the way that surveillance and incarceration technologies are implemented for profit by private firms, in collaboration with national and interstate agencies. As for the map of *European Norms*, it specifically charts the vast administrative structure that has arisen around the bureaucratic European Commission, whose directorates, innervated by the demands of corporate lobbies, produce the "industrial standards, territorial models, ideological guidelines and truth criteria" that help structure the production of a lifeworld—a steel-and concrete form of continental integration, vying with its distorting mirror in North America. *European Norms* also presents the interlocking structures of so-called "organized civil society," which serves to legitimate the status quo. But at the same time, with the lighter traceries of its mysterious, biomorphic front cover, devoted to "inklings of autonomy," it presents the patterns and meshworks of worldwide potentials for resistance.

These maps aspire to be cognitive tools, distributing as broadly as possible the kind of specialized information that was formerly confined to scholarly publications. Yet on another level they are meant to act as subjective shocks, energy potentials, informing the protest-performances as they are passed from hand to hand, deepening the resolve to resist as they are utilized in common or alone. In this sense it is the very closure of their intellectual discipline, the rigor of their conceptual effort to depict a totally administered world, that makes them *maps for the outside*, signs pointing to a territory that cannot yet be fully signified, and that will never be "represented" in the traditional ways. "Solidarity with extraterrestrials" reads one such indication, in an almost empty bubble at the lower left-hand corner of the cover of *European Norms*.

PERSPECTIVES

The acceleration of the last few years has been vertiginous, for everyone. Today, the accumulated knowledge of recent projects and the beginnings of a genuinely networked collaboration make it possible to envision more strategically focused mapping projects. Three recent studies—*Info war, Bio war, Psychic war*—respond to a need to grasp the fully military strategies of legitimation and population control that have emerged since 1989, with the end of the bipolar stasis predicated on the madness of mutual "overkill."[8] Similarly, more limited and precise maps of transnational state capitalism can now be imagined, attuned more closely to the possibilities of the protest and direct-action movements. Another perspective is the possible invention of a computer database, with a visual interface allowing the user to situate specific power-players within a nexus of supporting and opposing relations. Much remains to be done.

In this light, the old dilemma of the relation to gallery, magazine and museum structures fades toward insignificance. For the tactical media underground in Europe, art shows offer useful research deadlines, a chance to share ideas and critiques, at best some production money— and at worst, a damaging distraction. The revenge of the concept has been to finally create parallel and alternative circuits of experimentation, production, distribution, use and interpretation. To be sure, these circuits are hardly consolidated—but the best way to do so is to maintain other urgencies, which cannot be treated within any of the specialized subsystems.

Perhaps one such urgency can be expressed as a question, for artists and activists who must now address increasing levels of confrontation in the world. The question runs like this: Is it still possible to sublimate antagonistic conflicts into the transformative processes of reasoned, agonistic debate?[9] Or in other words: Can properly political relations be wrested from a totally administered world?

Notes

1. See Robert Barry, *Gallery Closing*, Amsterdam, Art & Project, December 17-31, Bulletin #17, in: Ursula Meyer, ed., *Conceptual Art* (New York: Dutton, 1972), p. 41.
2. Thanks to Andreas Broeckman for pointing my browser to a Howard Slater text that supports this definition. See the opening section of "The Spoiled Ideals of Lost Situations—Some Notes on Political Conceptual Art," at www.infopool.org.uk.
3. The journal M.A.U.S.S. ("Mouvement anti-utilitariste dans les sciences sociales") offers a look into some of the background ideas informing the debates over value in France after 1995.
4. See the Tangent University (www.u-tangente.org) for a far more precise overview, with texts on *gratuité totale* among many other subjects.
5. Those wishing to piece together the history of the Days of Global Action may consult the websites of People's Global Action and London Reclaim the Streets, among others.
6. The quote, from *Refuse the Biopolice*, applies to all the recent maps.
7. I refer to the famous phrase by Frederic Jameson, who in 1984 called for "an aesthetics of cognitive mapping" to resolve "the incapacity of our minds, at least at present, to map the great global multinational and decentered communicational network in which we find ourselves caught as individual subjects." See his essay, "Postmodernism, or the Cultural Logic of Late Capitalism," reprinted in the book under the same name.

8. Anyone with doubts about the epochal shift in military strategy after 1989 can consult John Arquilla and David Ronfeldt's books, such as *Networks and Netwars: The Future of Terror, Crime, and Militancy*, available as PDFs at www.rand.org/publications.
9. Antagonistic conflict refers to situations where one adversary must win and the other lose; agonistic debate supposes the possibility of an outcome acceptable to both parties. The distinction is made by Chantal Mouffe and Ernesto Laclau, in *Hegemony and Socialist Strategy*; those who get bored reading dense books can listen to the video of Mouffe's talk at the recent "Dark Markets" conference, available at http://darkmarkets.t0.or.at/programme.htm.

6

THE REVENGE OF THE CONCEPT

ARTISTIC EXCHANGES, NETWORKED RESISTANCE

I

Among the events of recent history, few have been as surprising, as full of enigmas, as the coordinated world demonstrations known as the Global Days of Action. Immediately upon their appearance, they overflowed the organization that had called them into being: the People's Global Action (PGA), founded in Geneva in February of 1998.[1] This transnational network of resistance had adopted a new concept of solidarity advanced by the Zapatistas, who encouraged everyone to take direct action at home, against the system of exploitation and oppression which they described as neoliberalism. As early as the month of May, 1998, the PGA helped spark demonstrations against the WTO whose effectiveness lay both in their simultaneity and in their extreme diversity: street parties in some thirty cities around the world, on May 16; four days of protest and rioting in Geneva, beginning that same day; a 50,000-strong march that reached Brasilia on May 20; protests all over India after a huge demonstration in Hyderabad against the WTO on May 2. The following year, London Reclaim the Streets launched the idea of a "carnival against capital" in financial centers across the world for the day of the G8 summit, June 18: there were actions in over forty cities, including a ten-thousand-strong "carnival of the oppressed" by Niger Delta peoples against transnational oil companies. In the face of transnational capitalism, a networked resistance was born, local and global, tactical and strategic: a new kind of political dissidence, self-organized and anarchist, diffusely interconnected and operating only from below, yet able to strike at the greatest concentrations of power. What is the strength of such movements? The unlikely appeal to a "do-it-yourself geopolitics": a chance for personal involvement in the transformation of the world.

These kinds of actions are about as far as one could imagine from a museum; yet when you approach them, you can feel something distinctly artistic. They bring together the multiplicity of individual expression and the unity of a collective will. That is their enigma, which sets up a circulation between singularity and solidarity, cooperation and freedom. But this enigma stretches further, into the paradoxes of a networked resistance. Because since their surprising beginnings, we have seen the movements change, we have seen them globalize. Activists from the South and the North travel across the earth in jet planes, to demonstrate next to people without money, without work, without land or papers—but who may know the same writers, the same philosophers, the same critiques of contemporary capitalism. The intensive use of Internet by the movement of movements means that dissenting messages take the pathways used by financial speculation. Sometimes you wonder whether the two can even be distinguished. What are the sources of this networked resistance? And what exactly is being resisted? Is revolution really the only option—as one could read on a banner at the carnival against capital, on June 18, 1999, in the financial center of London? Or do we not become what we resist? Are the "multitudes" the very origin and driving force of capitalist globalization, as some theorists believe?[2]

Two British critics, Anthony Davies and Simon Ford, posed exactly those questions, with direct reference to art. They pointed to the way that artistic practice was tending to integrate with London's financial economy, particularly through the vector of specially designed "culture clubs" where artists sought new forms of sponsorship and distribution, while businessmen looked for clues on how to restructure their hierarchical organizations into cooperative teams of creative, autonomous individuals: "We are witnessing the birth of an alliance culture that collapses the distinctions between companies, nation states, governments, private individuals—even the protest movement," the two critics claimed.[3] They drew a link between contemporary artistic experiments—those dealing with the use and appropriation of complex signs and tools, or with the catalysis of interactions between free individuals—and the politicized street parties of the late 1990s. But their analysis opposed these new movements, not to transnational capitalism, but to the outdated world of pyramid-shaped hierarchical organizations. Thus their image of the June 18 carnival: "On the one hand you have a networked coalition of semi-autonomous groups and on the other, the hierarchical command and control structure of the City of London police force. Informal networks are also replacing older political groups based on formal rules and fixed organizational structures and chains of command. The emergence of a decentralized transnational network-based protest movement represents a significant threat to those sectors that are slow in shifting from local and centralized hierarchical bureaucracies to flat, networked organizations."

Conceived at the outset of the year 2000, this alliance theory was mainly concerned with distinguishing a "new economy" from the old one. It combined a network paradigm of organization, as promoted by Manuel Castells,[4] with a description of the culturalization of the economy, as in British cultural studies. But what it demonstrated was more like an "economization of culture." Everything seemed to be swirling together: "In a networked culture, the topographical metaphor of 'inside' and 'outside' has become increasingly untenable. As all sectors loosen their physical structures, flatten out, form alliances and dispense with tangible centers, the oppositionality that has characterized previous forms of protest and resistance is finished as a useful model."

These kinds of remarks, which came from many quarters, were already confusing for the movements. But they took on an even more troubling light when the Al Qaeda network literally exploded into world consciousness. On the one hand, the unprecedented effectiveness of the S11 action seemed to prove the superiority of the networked paradigm over the command hierarchies associated with the Pentagon and the Twin Towers. But at the same time, if any position could be called "oppositional," it was now that of the Islamic fundamentalists. Their successful attack appeared to validate both the theory of a decisive transformation in organizational structures, and Samuel Huntington's theory of the "clash of civilizations." Suddenly the protest movement could identify neither with the revolutionary form of the network, nor with the oppositional refusal of the capitalist system. Loud voices from the right immediately seized the opportunity to assimilate the movement to terrorism. And to make matters worse, the financial collapse that the movement had predicted effectively happened, from the summer of 2000 onwards, casting suspicion over everything associated with the dot-com bubble—including all the progress in democratic communication. At the same time, the secret services of the most powerful countries, and especially the US, declared themselves ready to meet the challenge of the networks, by giving their forces new capacities for autonomy, horizontality, interlinkage.[5] The difficulty of situating a networked resistance to capitalism within a broader spectrum of social forces thus became enormous—as it still is today.

Now, this difficulty has not stopped the mobilizations, particularly in Europe. What has come to a halt, or rather, splintered into a state of extreme dispersal, are the theoretical attempts to explain them in a way that can contribute something both to their goals and to their capacities of self-organization. What I want to do here is to make a fresh try at this kind of explanation, from an anthropological viewpoint that can distinguish between the fictions of a "self-regulated market" and the reciprocities and solidarities that make it possible to live together as human beings. So we'll begin with a social and economic study of the vital need for resistance to the crises of capitalism. We will then see this resistance develop within the contemporary technical environment, without accepting any form of technological determinism. And finally, returning to the question of alliance or opposition, we can grasp some of the contributions that artistic practice makes to this networked resistance, by rediscovering languages that seemed to have been consigned to the museum. I am thinking primarily of conceptual art: a practice that doesn't produce works, but only virtualities, which can then be actualized, at each time and in each place, as unique performances.

II

Following the Zapatistas, people in the movement of movements tend to call the current economic structure "neoliberal." But this word evokes a political philosophy stretching back to the eighteenth century. One can speak instead of *flexible accumulation*, which describes the computer-linked, finance-driven, just-in-time model of the globalized economy.[6] By subordinating the other spheres of social life—education, science, culture, etc.—this organization of production and consumption produces a veritable hegemony, a mode of regulation for society as a whole. To grasp the way this hegemony is experienced by individuals, I have proposed the notion of the *flexible personality*.[7] It is an ambiguous notion, because it designates both the managerial culture that legitimates the globalized economy, and renders it tolerable or even attractive for those who are its privileged subjects, as well as the "flexible" nature of a workforce that is subject to increasingly individualized forms of exploitation. In other words, the flexible personality designates the lived experience of a relation of domination. It has become essential to define the limits of that relation.

One can begin to do so by pointing to the different kinds of social struggles that have intensified over the last ten years. Ecological struggles, against resource waste, polluting industry, invasive infrastructures. Workers' struggles, against falling wages, worsening labor conditions, insufficient health coverage or unemployment benefits. Struggles against the privatization of medical and scientific knowledge, against the control of the university and of cultural production by business. And finally, struggles against the preponderance of the financial sphere in the taking of democratic decisions. This list of different fields of struggle refers us, in a more abstract way, to four "fictious commodities": land, labor, knowledge and money itself. That is, four major articulations of social life which capitalism claims to treat as things to be sold, confiding their destiny to the operations of a self-regulating market.[8] The problem being that the basic conditions under which these "things" are produced do not all have a price tag, and so escape any monetary regulation. These four major articulations of society exist at least partially outside the market: they are "externalities."[9] And the maintenance of their fictive status as commodities implies a perpetually deferred cost, which in the long run can only manifest itself in a phenomenon outside any imaginable accounting. This is the phenomenon of systemic crisis. Its looming shadow has motivated the increasing levels of social struggle.

It was an anthropologist, Karl Polanyi, who provided the most striking description of a systemic crisis, in a book called *The Great Transformation*, published in 1944. The story begins with the enclosure of community pasture lands in England, known as *commons*, which were transformed with fences into private property. This privatization of resources led to the appearance of rural poverty in the course of the eighteenth century. The threat of famine then made possible an unprecedented exploitation of labor power, which former peasants were compelled to sell for a bare minimum in the new factories of the Industrial Revolution. In this way, the owning class accumulated great fortunes, which split away from the nationally instituted money to employ the international currency of gold bullion. Polanyi pays special attention to the directive role that independent bankers played in the creation of the gold standard, which served as a universal, but legally private equivalent between all the different national currencies. He shows that a cycle of three privatizations—land, labor, and money—leads finally to the worldwide market of the nineteenth century.

For a hundred years, gold served as a coherent and relatively stable language of exchange for commercial transactions; and the profits were a powerful argument in favor of peace, or at least, against generalized warfare. It was the gradual abandonment of the international gold standard under the pressure of repeated financial breakdowns that led, in the 1930s, to the reconstitution of strictly national economies, closed in on themselves and subject to various forms of central planning (ranging from the relatively benign New Deal, to Nazism and Stalinism). But Polanyi, writing in 1944, did not suggest anything as simplistic as restoring the gold standard. His strongest argument was that the violence of free-market exchanges, when "disembedded" from their place within the larger social structure of reciprocities and solidarities, was finally what destroyed the laissez-faire system itself, provoking the fascist reaction. The fundamental problem therefore lay with the very notion of the self-regulating market. The last chapter of *The Great Transformation* predicts the opening of a new era in the history of humanity. It calls for the institution of a mixed economy, broadly regulated within a national framework and yet also highly respectful of individual rights, able to guarantee what the author describes as "freedom in a complex society"—that is, in a society which has recognized the limits of the free market

The model of the Keynesian welfare state that was installed in the industrially developed countries during the post-war period could appear as an answer to Polanyi's vision. It submitted industrial and financial activity to a social regulation, conceived within each national framework in a more or less democratic fashion. But the dynamics of capitalism—which are historically inseparable from those of imperialism—rapidly overflowed this national frame, as one can see in the evolution of the world monetary system. After the war, the Bretton Woods treaty tied signatory countries into a system of relatively stable exchange rates, whereby all the currencies were pegged to the dollar, which in turn was convertible into gold. But this system proved untenable, and after the United States suspended convertibility in 1971, the currencies began to "float" against each other; since the outset of the eighties they have been subject to the fluctuations of a highly speculative exchange market, operating at the speed of computers and telecommunications. At the same time, controls on crossborder investments have gradually been lifted, and many state services and industries, considered as unfair competition with the private sector, have been suppressed. In a world which no longer erects any significant barriers to the directive capacity of money, capital flow into the stock markets now commands the majority of productive investments everywhere; and every material reality comes to be dependent on highly volatile financial information. In this way there arises what Rem Koolhaas has called "the world of ¥ / € / $": a world-economy built around the incessantly changing equivalence of the yen, the euro, and the dollar, representing the three major poles of world prosperity. One can see the convertibility of these three currencies as a new kind of economic language, serving primarily to convey the opportunistic speech of private investors, indeed, of a transnational capitalist class. ¥ / € / $ is the monetary language of the flexible personality.

The last twenty years have seen the incredible inventiveness of this worldwide language, which has generated a myriad of private dialects: stocks, futures, options, swaptions, floaters, hedges, and so on through the endless list of derivatives. Despite their appearance of total autonomy, of absolute disconnection from the solid earth, these forms of privately managed credit money have directed the productive apparatus of the world's countries, ever more radically since 1989. In parallel to these developments in the private sphere, a new type of postnational state has slowly come into being, abandoning the former emphasis on social security and public welfare, and seeking instead to encourage the insertion of its most innovative citizens into the worldwide information economy.[10] And the language of ¥ / € / $ has also taken on cultural, intellectual, organizational and imaginary forms, giving rise to artistic productions, managerial techniques, modes of behaviors, desires and dreams that have served to legitimate the regime of flexible accumulation, while continually feeding it with new innovations. But this very inventiveness, this speculative confidence, has also gnawed away at the ecological, social, political, and financial foundations of the system. We went through the Asian crisis of 1997, which spread to Russia and Brazil, threatening even the American economy; then we saw the krach of the NASDAQ in spring 2000, sparking a two-year plunge of the world's stock markets (which remain extremely volatile at the date of writing, three years later). The possibility of a systemic crisis, which could be seen on the horizon throughout the 1990s, has rushed suddenly closer at the outset of the new millennium.

What are the effects of the crisis as it stands today? One can draw a few insights from recent developments in Argentina. In the late 1990s the Argentine state, under pressure from the IMF, desperately attempted to maintain the value of the peso with respect to the dollar, and more broadly, with respect to the globalized standard of prosperity represented by the currencies of ¥ / € / $. A series of structural adjustments were supposed to improve the economy's health, and insure the parity of the peso and the dollar; but their effect was to exclude increasing numbers of Argentines from access to employment, basic services, food, and finally even to their money, when bank withdrawals were frozen in late November 2001. Thus the state's maintenance of the peso's exchange value, ensuring the integration of the country's elite to the world economy, no longer permitted any use value on the local level. Resistance now became a question of sheer survival, and some Argentines spoke of a crisis in the very process of civilization: "The new state project implies, in the short term, an abrupt cut-off... of the systems of social reproduction: the state gradually detaches itself from the populations and the territories; and finally, from social cohesion itself."[11] But this detachment only gives the state the power of an empty affirmation, an entirely formal language of exchange, which is valid in theory but not in fact. And the void calls out either for a democratic invention, or for an authoritarian solution.

This situation of suspended crisis appears likely to spread, leaving open, at least for a time, the possibility of very different responses. The illusions of the 1990s, however, are definitely over. The collapse of the stock markets, and the economic slowdown that has followed, brings a threat of deflation, unemployment and exclusion to bear on most of the world's populations. Under current political conditions, the only possible response seems to be a strengthening of the barriers that separate the privileged classes from all the others—and this, even within the richest countries. The new military posture of the United States, while directly motivated by the September 11 attacks, also represents an attempt to restructure society, and to institute a new form of discipline in the face of the void that has been left by the collapse of the speculative bubble. It is in this way that the ideological version of economic flexibility meets its own limits. This shift toward heightened military and police control takes away much of the legitimacy that flexible modes of management were able to confer on capitalist society. Still the opportunistic model of the flexible personality will probably continue to orient the behavior of privileged individuals for years yet to come, even as it subjects them to strong contradictions. Under such conditions, the various forms of resistance to capitalism will clearly intensify, not least because they find a vital energy in the feeling of absolute necessity brought on by the crisis. Now I want to deal specifically with one such form of resistance: the resistance to the privatization of knowledge, the fourth "fictitious commodity" whose importance Polanyi had not yet measured. It is through the cooperative production of immaterial knowledge that we will rejoin the enigma of the networked protests.

Just one more thing. I do not want to accord any privilege, in what follows, to that supposedly more "advanced" fraction of the world population which is so deeply involved with electronic networks. I think the opposition between the "Net" and "Self"—between a modernizing process that enforces our abstraction from historical and cultural traditions, or failing that, determines a desperate and regressive retreat to the fixations of local identity—is simply false.[12] More interesting is the divide between the possessive individualism of the flexible personality, and a concern for human coexistence. As we saw above, the movement of movements found one of its beginnings in a concept of solidarity arising from the Zapatista struggles, which have fundamentally to do with questions of land. But the meaning of these survival struggles of the Mayan peoples could only reach the subjects of the developed world through the Internet, where the commodification of cultural and scientific knowledge is at stake. Here the essential struggle is to overtake and dissolve the language of ¥ / € / $, not through a return to the closed, bureaucratic frameworks of the Keynesian state, but instead through the *political* development of new principles of exchange and reciprocity. Thus this fourth field of resistance, with touches closely on human language but also on technical development, seems destined to furnish elements of articulation for other struggles, in a shared search for alternatives to the systemic crisis.

III

It is well known that the Linux operating-system kernel, and free software generally, is made cooperatively without any money changing hands. This is something that quickly caught the attention of artists and culture critics, as in the discussions over what Richard Barbrook called the "high-tech gift economy."[13] The expression recalls an anthropologist, not Polanyi but Marcel Mauss, the author of the famous essay, *The Gift*. His essential contribution was to underscore, at the very heart of modern economic exchange, the presence of motives irreducible to the calculation of the value of material objects, and also of the individual interest one might have in possessing them. As Barbrook points out, the heritage of Mauss was very much alive in alternative circles, his ideas having inspired the Situationists, who passed them on to the do-it-yourself media ethic of the Punk movement. But mostly what fueled the discussion of the Internet gift economy was not theory, but the simple practice of adding information to the net. As Rishab Aiyer Ghosh explained, "the economy of the Net begins to look like a vast tribal cooking-pot, surging with production to match consumption, simply because everyone understands —instinctively, perhaps— that trade need not occur in single transactions of barter, and that one product can be exchanged for millions at a time. The cooking-pot keeps boiling because people keep putting in things as they themselves, and others, take things out."[14] By placing the accent on the overflowing abundance and free nature of the available content, Ghosh responded implicitly to one of the most contested themes in Mauss's essay, which cast each gift as the deliberate imposition of a debt on the receiver, instating hierarchies which were quite foreign to the practice of networked information exchange.

Today, with the popular explosion of BitTorrent and other peer-to-peer file-sharing systems, these notions of the high-tech gift economy have begun to form part of common sense. It seems to admit at least a few new things: that the coded creations circulating on the Internet are never "consumed" like a cigarette would be; that use by some people in no way limits their availability for others; and that certain kinds of exchanges therefore have nothing to do with rarity and are quite possible without money. What is less often remarked, because of a denial which is characteristic of free-market rhetoric, is the fact that non-monetary models of exchange have been operating on a very large scale for as long as one can remember, for instance in the realm of academic publishing, where the primary motive for sharing information is not its monetary value but the recognition it brings—a recognition which itself is at least partially dependent on the idea of contributing something to humanity or truth. In fact there exists quite a large movement in the domain of scientific publishing aiming for online release of all the articles carried by specialized journals, in order to make the results universally accessible despite the increasing cost of many essential print publications.[15] Recently, an author by the name of Yochai Benkler has taken the twin examples of free software and academic publishing as a foundation on which to build a general theory of what he calls "commons-based peer production," by which he means non-proprietary informational or cultural production, based on materials which are extremely low cost or inherently free. This voluntary form of self-organized production depends, in his words, "on very large aggregations of individuals independently scouring their information environment in search of opportunities to be creative in small or large increments. These individuals then self-identify for tasks and perform them for complex motivational reasons."[16] Benkler's first aim, however, is not to explain peoples' motivation, but simply to describe the organizational and technological conditions that make this cooperative production possible.

Four attributes of the networked information economy appear as preconditions of commons-based peer production. First, information must be freely available as inexhaustible raw material for products which, in their turn, will become inexhaustible raw materials for further productions. Second, potential collaborators must be easily able to find the project that inspires them to creativity and labor. Third, the cost of production equipment must be low, as is now the case for things like computers and related media devices. Fourth, it must be possible to broadly distribute the results, for instance, over a telecommunications net. Under these conditions, quite complex tasks can be imagined, divided into small modules, and thrown out into the public realm where individuals will self-identify their competency to meet any given challenge. The only remaining requirement for large-scale production of cultural and informational goods is to be able to perform quality checks and integrate all the individual modules with relatively low effort into a completed whole—but these tasks, it turns out, can often be done on a distributed basis as well. The fact that all of this is possible, and actually happening today, allows Benkler to contradict Ronald Coase's classic theory, which identifies the firm, with its hierarchical command structure, and the market, functioning through the individual's quest for the lowest price, as the only two viable ways to organize human production. In other words, in the cultural and informational domain there is an alternative mode of production, functioning outside the norms of the state-capitalist economy as we know it, but without any rhetorical need to proclaim a clean break or an absolute division between them.

The notion of the commons refers back to the same pre-capitalist history that Polanyi had invoked; and it does so in the context of what some are calling the "second enclosure movement," resulting in the extension of intellectual property rights, or the privatization of information. Benkler stresses that the word "commons" denotes "the *absence of exclusion* as the organizing feature of this new mode of production." To be sure, the examples he uses to prove the existence of voluntarily organized large-scale cultural production are strictly electronic projects like the Wikipedia encyclopedia, the Slashdot technews site, the Kuro5hin site, and so on. These are essentially situations where publicly available text plus creativity produces more publicly available text. They are also politically neutral examples, appropriate for an argumentation that aims, among other things, to influence the American legislature on the subject of copyright laws. Yet one could apply exactly the same ideas to the growing phenomenon of networked political protests. It is clear that mass access to email and the possibility to create personal web pages—both of which have been integral to the world expansion of liberal capitalism—almost immediately made possible, not only a greater awareness of globalization and its effects, but also the self-organization of dissenting movements on a world scale. And the scope of the projects that have been realized in this sense has been tremendous.

Just reflect for a moment on what each of the major "counter-globalization" actions has involved. Collaborative research on the political, social, cultural, and ecological issues at stake. Various levels of coordination between a wide range of already constituted groups, concerning the preliminary forms of mobilization. Worldwide dissemination, through every possible channel, of the research and preliminary positions. Travel of tens or hundreds of thousands of single persons and autonomous groups to a given place. Self-organization of meeting and sleeping places. Intellectual and political cooperation on some form of counter-summit. The creation of artistic and cultural events in the spirit of the movements. A minimal agreement, worked out beforehand or in the heat of the moment, on the specific forms and places of the symbolic and direct actions to be undertaken. Legal and medical coordination in order to ensure the demonstrators' security. The installation of communications systems allowing for the transmission of precise yet exceedingly diverse coverage of the events. A social, legal, and political follow-up of the aftermath. Finally, a subsequent analysis of the new situation that results from each confrontation: in other words, a new starting-point.

In this sense one could say that, just like the projects of commons-based peer production, these mobilizations begin and end with the fabrication of publicly available texts. For example, the People's Summit in Quebec City in April 2001 began long in advance, with many different studies of the consequences to be expected from the future agreement on the Free Trade Area of the Americas. These studies led to the drafting of a remarkable document, "Alternatives for the Americas," which is a counter-treaty of great precision, composed through a process of knowledge exchange and political coordination on the scale of the American hemisphere.[17] It's also true that as a direct consequence of the massive demonstration that took place during the summit, the official working draft of the FTAA treaty was made public for the first time; until then it had not even been available to elected representatives of the American peoples, but only to executive negotiating teams (and scores of corporate "advisers"). In this way the counter-globalization movements constitute a public archive. And yet between the fundamental landmarks represented by these text publications, how many face-to-face debates took place, how many moments of singular or collective creation, how many acts of courage and solidarity? And how many emotions, images, memories, and desires were created and shared during the days of action in Quebec City?

The spectacle of these great gatherings, overflowing with freely given creations, could appear like a new form of the potlatch ceremonies described by Marcel Mauss, a gift-giving ritual where the demonstrators try to outdo their adversaries through open displays of generosity. No doubt there is something of that, which explains why the words "free" and "priceless" have been so important in these demonstrations. But what seems more interesting in the reference to Mauss is his way of perceiving gift-giving rituals as "total social facts," bringing all the different aspects of social life together in a system of complex and indivisible relations. Whoever saw the extraordinary symbolic transactions between pacifists, ecologists, unionists, anarchists, spirtualists, delinquents, reporters, by-passers, cops and politicians at the G8 summit in Genoa, in July of 2001, can find a real resonance in what Mauss says about the Melanesian gift-giving ceremonies, the American Indian potlatch rituals, and the "market-festivals of the Indo-European world":

> All these phenomena are at once legal, economic, religious, and even aesthetic, morphological, etc. They are legal, including public and private law, diffuse and organized morality; they are strictly obligatory or simply praised and blamed, political and domestic at the same time, involving the social classes as well as the clans and families. They are religious: including strict religion and magic and animism and diffuse religious mentality. They are economical: because the idea of value, of utility, of interest, of luxury, of wealth, of acquisition and accumulation as well as consumption and even purely sumptuary expenditure are everywhere in them, even though these are all understood differently than by us today. What is more, these institutions have an important aesthetic side to them... the dances that are carried out alternatively, the chants and parades of all kinds, the dramatic performances... everything, food, objects, and services, even "respect," as the Tlingits say, everything is a cause for aesthetic emotion.[18]

There is no nostalgia for a primitive life in the fact of quoting Mauss, nor any facile admiration for the "revolutionary fête." Things are much more complex. On the one hand, the contemporary quest for "direct action," for "direct democracy," finds an initial realization in the collective, cooperative production of these public events, which bring together all the rigorously separated aspects of modern social life. Indeed, the very aim of such events is to criticize certain fundamental separations, like the one that amputates any basic concern for life from the laws of monetary accumulation. But that doesn't mean that the event, the ecstatic convergence, is a total solution: instead it is a departure point for a fresh questioning of the social tie, at times when its deadly aspects become visible, as they are today. The protesters' claim, not just to the occupation but to the *creation* of public space, with all the conflicts it brings in its wake, offers society an occasion to theatricalize the real, in order to replay the meaning of abstractions that are no longer adequate to the needs and possibilities of life. The "total social fact" of the contemporary demonstration is, at its best, a chance to relearn and recreate a language for political debate, which isn't just about money, and doesn't only have "¥ / € / $" in its vocabulary. And the networked protests we are speaking of, including those of the peace movement in 2003, have produced the first chances to do this at the scale of the globalized economy and of global governance.

Artistic practice has been one of the keys to the emergence of these "global social facts"—not least because artistic practice has also been one of the ways to hold off group violence, to open up a theatrical space that doesn't immediately become a war zone. This is obviously something that contemporary society risks forgetting, and that particular risk is reason enough in itself to go beyond the specialized, disciplinary definition of art, to try to relocate art within a much broader political economy. Before I do that, however, I want to draw one last group of ideas from Yochai Benkler. His paper closes with the problem of what he calls "threats to motivation." One of these comes from the failure to integrate the results of commons-based peer production into usable wholes which can make a project successful. Translated into political terms, this would mean the failure of the networked movements to change any tangible aspect of social life. That is a real threat to motivation; and I think it's vitally important to keep offering practical ideas and proposals about possible changes on all the scales of governance and existence, from the neighborhood to the world level, at every new demonstration. Benkler points to different strategies for putting together the results of common effort. These strategies range from self-organization of the integration process, to the delegation of this tricky point to hierarchical structure or to a commercial enterprise. Again the translation into our terms is obvious, and has become increasingly visible at events such as the first European Social Forum, held in Florence in November of 2002. Just when the networked struggles get big enough to succeed, there is an enormous temptation to hand them over, in the name of efficiency, to a traditional politburo supported by professional media people. The problem with such expedient strategies is that they risk giving participants the impression that the voluntary production of political culture with their peers is being confiscated by somebody in a directive position. A fantastic example of this is the thirty-thousand member ATTAC association in France, which, to many members discontent, is in fact a strictly controlled, hierarchical organization at the national level. However, for ATTAC to have the social power it does, it has had to also produce a decentralized network of local committees, which operate very differently from the national bureau and regularly criticize or contradict its decisions. The tension you can see there in a very real situation, between collective process and effective decision, is at the heart of the democratic experiment today. You might even say that working though that kind of tension is the art of politics.

IV

So now we return to the language of art, and to an art whose very essence is language. Obviously I'm talking about conceptual art. But today this most revolutionary of all art forms is considered a failure. The "escape strategies" that Lucy Lippard talks about in her famous book on *The Dematerialization of the Art Object* were intended to free artists from dependency on the gallery-magazine-museum circuit. It was thought that artists could motivate people to use their imagination in completely new ways, by giving them linguistic suggestions, virtual proposals that they could actualize outside the specialized institutions. But exclusive signatures rapidly took precedence over the infinite permutation of the works in the lives of the viewers/users. The necessary corollary of the signature was that the concept should refer primarily to itself, as in a famous piece composed of a chair, a picture of a chair, and a dictionary definition of the word "chair" (Joseph Kosuth, *One and Three Chairs*, 1965). Such a work, completing itself in a tautology that required no transformative activity from the public, could easily be presented within the existing system. Thus the conceptual escape attempt only led from market-oriented New York to the museums of Europe, then finally back to the market. In 1973, Seth Siegelaub said in an interview: "Conceptual art, more than all previous types of art, questions the fundamental nature of art. Unhappily, the question is strictly limited to the exclusive domain of the fine arts. There is still the potential of it authorizing an examination of all that surrounds art, but in reality, conceptual artists are dedicated only to exploring avant-garde aesthetic problems.... The economic pattern associated with conceptual art is remarkably similar to that of other artistic movements: to purchase a work cheap and resell it at a high price. In short, speculation."[19] Lucy Lippard, for her part, wrote in 1973 that the "ghetto mentality predominant in the narrow and incestuous art world... with its reliance on a very small group of dealers, curators, editors and collectors who are all too frequently and often unknowingly bound by invisible apron strings to the 'real world's' power structures... make[s] it unlikely that conceptual art will be any better equipped to affect the world any differently than, or even as much as, its less ephemeral counterparts."[20]

These admissions of defeat are well known.[21] But in certain recent publications, another history of conceptual art has been coming back to light. It is a history that unfolds in Latin America, and particularly in Argentina, in the cities of Buenos Aires and Rosario. It would seem that here, in the context of an authoritarian government and under the pressure of American cultural imperialism, conceptual art could only be received—or invented—as an invitation to act antagonistically within the mass-media sphere. Certain Argentine pop artists considered that the commercial news media could actually be appropriated as an artistic medium, like a canvas or a gallery space. To do this, Roberto Jacoby and Eduardo Costa created an artificial happening, one that never really happened, and they stimulated the media with information about it, so as to achieve specific fictional effects.[22] But this attempt was only a first step towards a fully political appropriation of the communications media by artists. The most characteristic project was *Tucumán Arde*, or "Tucumán is Burning," realized in 1968.[23] The military government was attempting to "modernize" the sugar-cane industry in the province of Tucumán, with a shift of scale toward larger factories under the control of local oligarchs and foreign capital; at the same time, the official media painted an idyllic picture of a region which in reality was wracked by impoverishment and intense labor struggles. So a group of some thirty artists and sociologists from Buenos Aires and Rosario began researching the social and economic conditions in the province, carrying out an analysis of all the mass-media coverage of the region, and going out themselves to gather first-hand information and to document the situation using photography and film. They then staged an exhibition that was explicitly designed to feed their work back into the national debate, so as to counter the media picture. Yet the project, although it did not shy away from advertising techniques, could not be reduced to counter-propaganda. As Andrea Giunta writes:

> In many of its characteristic traits—such as the exploration of the interaction between languages, the centrality of the activity required from the spectator, the unfinished character, the importance of the documentation, the dissolution of the idea of the author, and the questioning of the art system and the ideas that legitimate it—Tucumán Arde maintains a relation with the repertory of conceptual art. But not with the tautological and self-referential form of conceptualism, in which, from a certain viewpoint, one finds a reconfirmation of the modernist paradigm. Language does not refer back to language, to the specificity of the artistic fact; instead, the contextual relations are so strong in this case that reality ceases being understood as a space of reflection and comes to be conceived as a possible field of action oriented toward the transformation of society.24

Tucumán Arde is extremely interesting to consider from the contemporary viewpoint of tactical media practice, which in many respects has been one long effort to research, expose, and go beyond the idyllic picture of globalization being painted by the corporate media.25 But to understand the major differences from today's situation, one must realize that *Tucumán Arde* was done with the support of the Argentine CGT, that is, a radical labor union, and the exhibition was shown in a union hall. In other words, to obtain the funding and distribution of practices that would not be supported by the market, the Rosario group had to collaborate with a bureaucratic structure, which is defined by its relation to the capitalist firm. And that kind of cooperation is almost impossible today, at least in the overdeveloped countries. For reasons which have to do both with the anti-bureaucratic bias of the New Left, and with the heightened integration of labor unions to the state after the crisis of 1968, it has become very difficult for social movements, let alone artists, to collaborate with official structures such as parties, unions, etc. The motivation just isn't there. This is why the use of carefully conceived linguistic formulas, of oriented but open signifiers, would become a far more effective means of mobilization in the late 1990s, when ideas could be distributed and constantly transformed through the proliferation of connections offered by the Internet. In this way one achieved a non-bureaucratic capacity for subversive political action on a large scale, outside any compulsory framework. A new kind of conceptualism began to emerge, in which "attitudes become forms," as the curator Harald Szeeman had said in the 1960s. An idea or phrase could become a world-wide event, in which every individual performance was different. Just as in Lawrence Weiner's famous prescription, the action could be carried out by the originators of the ideas, or realized by others, or not done at all. In the late 1990s, this revolutionary promise was realized. Thirty years after experiments such as *Tucumán Arde*, the counter-globalization movement burst onto the world scene as the revenge of the concept.

The examples of this could be as numerous as there are experiences. That is why I want to talk about an event in which I was personally involved: the carnivalesque performance and riot in the City of London on June 18, 1999. Before it took place, this day was intensely dreamed by a multiplicity of actors, sometimes connected in constant dialogue and exchange, sometimes affected at a distance by signs that promised to break their isolation and unleash their agency. The inspiration first emerged, at least in certain versions of the story, during the summer of 1998 in conversations between members of London Reclaim the Streets and the anarchist group London Greenpeace (not the famous NGO).[26] It spread through the networks of Peoples' Global Action, drawing on the suggestive potency of two key ideas. One was the "street party," as a form of direct democracy which refused the domination of the city by the automobile, but also the traditional procedures of party politics. The other was the phrase "Our resistance is as transnational as capital": a return of twentieth-century internationalism in red, black, and green, after a long trip through the jungles of Chiapas where the Zapatista uprising began on January 1, 1994 (the day NAFTA came into effect). A complex circulation through time and space, where solidarity means respect for local autonomy and differing motivations for struggle, was encapsulated in these two key ideas. A call to action, circulated widely through the Internet, put it like this:

> The proposal is to encourage as many movements and groups as possible to organize their own autonomous protests or actions, on the same day (June 18th), in the same geographical locations (financial/ corporate/ banking/ business districts) around the world. Events could take place at relevant sites, e.g. multinational company offices, local banks, stock exchanges. Each event would be organized autonomously and coordinated in each city or financial district by a variety of movements and groups. It is hoped that a whole range of different groups will take part, including workers, peasants, indigenous peoples, women, students, the landless, environmentalists, unwaged/unemployed and others.... everyone who recognizes that the global capitalist system, based on the exploitation of people and the planet for the profit of a few, is at the root of our social and ecological troubles.[27]

J18 in London was the most exquisitely planned and spontaneously realized artistic performance in which I have ever taken part, an awakening to new possibilities of political struggle that would be echoed throughout the world. Thousands converged in the morning at the Liverpool tube station in the City, receiving carnival masks in four different colors that encouraged the crowd to split into groups, outwitting the police by following different paths through the medieval street plan of Europe's largest financial district, then coming together again in front of the LIFFE building, the London International Financial Futures and Options Exchange, which was the symbolic and real target of this protest against the global domination of speculative capital. The choice of site was essential. Long years of effort by far-flung organizers and intellectuals had been required to understand and describe the ways in which capital had escaped its former national bounds, in order to redeploy itself transnationally in new oppressive systems; yet until the late 1990s, that knowledge remained largely abstract, floating in a deterritorialized space like the financial sphere itself. Here it was translated into tangible forms of embodied expression: transgressive dancing, defiant music, a verbal and visual poetics of resistance. For once, individual pleasure once did not appear as the negation, but rather as the accentuation of collective struggle, confronting financial abstractions which could be understood by the participants through the immediate experience of the stone-and-glass architecture, while the significance of each of their acts was multiplied by the knowledge that other, similar events were occurring all over the planet. Spontaneous invitations for passing traders to come join the party were combined with sudden attacks on private property, generating an unexpected, threatening, sympathetic and immensely confident image of revolt—a way to finally start answering the decades-old pleas for help from oppressed peoples in the South, while also responding to the unbearable social divisions that transnational capitalism imposes on countries like Britain. Of course this carnivalesque outburst was just one moment in a longer process of struggle, prepared by untold numbers of people under far harsher conditions. But the language of protest that emerged here nonetheless marked a turning point. It was the immediate inspiration for the larger and more complex confrontation in Seattle, six months later, which finally forced the messages of the global resistance movements through the frosty screens of the traditional media, opening the political crisis of global capitalism's legitimacy. A crisis which has not ceased to morph and mutate into the increasingly violent forms that it is taking today.

From my point of view there can be no mistake. The revenge of the concept is the reappearance, in broad daylight, of the global class struggle: a political struggle over to right to share in the fruits of technological development, and to guard against its many poisons. But if this re-embodiment of class struggle can also be an artistic experience—and an experiment that reverses and transforms the concept of art—it is because the articulation of the old divides has radically changed. In the face of an all-dominating capitalist class which has imposed a global division of labor, and extended its ideological grip over core populations through the devices of popular stockholding, speculative pension funds, and the seductive traps of consumer credit, the focus of struggle is no longer so much the rate of the industrial wage, as the very existence and production of that which lies outside the cash nexus: land in the sense of a viable ecology; labor as the energy of life from its beginnings in travails of birth; knowledge not as fragmented commodities but as an overarching question about meaning; trade and exchange as an institution of human coexistence. Arising within these fields of struggle are new desires and political designs, irreducible to the organizing schemes of capital and state. In the best of cases, opposition becomes a prelude to radical invention.

Still the tensions have increased dramatically in all these domains, under the advancing pressure of systemic crisis. As the techniques of mass-mediated control ratchet up toward overt fascism, in the wake both of September 11 and of the stock market failures, the improbable meeting of teamsters and turtles in Seattle and the naked life dancing in front of the LIFFE building in London might seem to recede into some distant past. It is certain that the power of surprise was soon lost, as every international summit became an overwhelming protest, and the ruling oligarchies found new courage to ignore the democratic expressions of the citizens. Broader and deeper revolts must now be invented. But these were among the early experiments in a rearticulation of struggles, whose destiny is to cross all the borders. For the artists of another world, wherever they live and however they understand themselves, let these moments be counted among the hieroglyphs of the future.

Notes

Thanks to participants of the WorldInfo Con in Amsterdam, December 2002, for ideas, and to Felix Stalder, Ken Wark and Keith Hart, for critiques of an initial version circulated on the electonic mailinglist Nettime.

1. There is as yet no "history" of these ongoing movements, but information and stories can be found at www.agp.org.
2. This is the thesis of Negri and Hardt's *Empire* (Harvard University Press, 2000); also see Yoshihiko Ichida, "Questions d'Empire," *Multitudes* 7, December 2001, online at http://multitudes.samizdat.net/article.php3?id_article=54.

3. Anthony Davies and Simon Ford, "Art Networks," www.societyofcontrol.com/research/davis_ford.htm. Further quotes are from this article and "Culture Clubs," www.infopool.org.uk/cclubs.htm.
4. Manuel Castells, *The Rise of the Network Society* (Oxford: Blackwell, 1996).
5. The "Terrorism Information Awareness System," formerly described at www.darpa.mil/iao/TIASystems.htm, has since been defunded by the US Congress. For comprehensive information on the pursuit of mass surveillance techniques, see the report of the International Campaign Against Mass Surveillance, at www.i-cams.org.
6. Cf. David Harvey, *The Condition of Postmodernity* (Oxford: Blackwell, 1990), pp. 141–48.
7. Cf. Brian Holmes, "The Flexible Personality," *Hieroglyphs of the Future* (Zagreb: Arkzin/WHW, 2003), online at www.u-tagente.org.
8. Cf. Bob Jessop, *The Future of the Capitalist State* (Cambridge: Polity, 2002), pp. 12–14. In specific relation to money (which is sold massively as a commodity on international currency markets Jessop notes: "Money's ability to perform its economic functions depends critically on extra-economic institutions, sanctions and personal and impersonal trust. Insofar as money circulates as national money, the state has a key role in securing a formally rational monetary system; conversely, its increasing circulation as stateless money poses serious problems regarding the re-regulation of monetary relations" (p. 14).
9. For example, a government "Superfund" program was deemed necessary in the United States in 1980, to clean up toxic waste on land that companies had used as free dumping grounds. Since 1995 corporate taxation for this fund has been stopped, and since 2002 the Bush administration, hostile to the expense, is curtailing Federal funding. As though the ecological balance were at once priceless and impossible to pay for.
10. Cf. Jessop's treatment of the "Schumpeterian workforce postnational regime," in *The Future of the Capitalist State, op. cit.*
11. Colectivo Situaciones, *19 y 20: Apuntes sobre el nuevo protagonismo social* (Buenos Aires, De Mano en Mano, 2002).
12. The opposition between the self and the net structures Manuel Castells' three-volume work on the "information age"; it is dis-

cussed in the prologue to *The Rise of the Network Society, op. cit.*, pp. 1–28, and returns throughout the second volume, *The Power of Identity* (Oxford: Blackwell, 1997).
13. Richard Barbrook, "The Hi-Tech Gift Economy," in *ReadMe,* Filtered by Nettime (New York: Autonomedia, 1999), text online at www.firstmonday.dk/issues/issue3_12/barbrook.
14. Rishab Aiyer Ghosh, "Cooking Pot Economy," in *ReadMe, op. cit.,* online at www.firstmonday.dk/issues/issue3_3/ghosh/index.html#SEC5.
15. See, for example, the Budapest Open Access Initiative, www.soros.org/openaccess.
16. Yochai Benkler, "Coase's Penguin, or Linux and the Nature of the Firm," www.benkler.org/CoasesPenguin.html.
17. "Alternatives for the Americas," www.web.net/comfront/alts4americas/eng/eng.html.
18. Marcel Mauss, *Essai sur le don* (1923–24).
19. Michel Claura and Seth Siegelaub, "L'art conceptuel," in *Conceptual Art: A Critical Anthology,* eds. A. Alberro and B. Stimson (Cambridge, Mass.: MIT Press, 1999), pp. 289-90.
20. Lucy Lippard, "Postface," *Six Years: The Dematerialization of the Art Object from 1966 to 1972* (New York: Praeger, 1973), p. 264.
21. Cf. E. Costa, R. Escari, R. Jacoby, "A Media Art (Manifesto)," in *Conceptual Art: A Critical Anthology, op. cit.,* pp. 2-3.
22. For the classic example, see Benjamin Buchloh's assertion that conceptual art failed "to liberate the world from mythical forms of perception and hierarchical modes of specialized experience," and was "transformed into absolute farce." "Conceptual Art 1962–1969," *October,* Winter 1990, 143.
23. A description of *Tucumán Arde* (including the relation to Jacoby's work) can be found in Marí Carmen Ramírez, "Thriving on Adversity: Conceptualism in Latin America, 1960–1980," in *Global Conceptualism: Points of Origin, 1950s–1980s,* exhibition catalogue, Queens Museum of Art, 1999, pp. 66–67. Also see M.T. Gramuglio and N. Rosa, "Tucumán Burns," in *Conceptual Art: A Critical Anthology, op. cit.,* pp. 76–79.
24. Andrea Giunta, *Vanguardia, internacionalismo y política: arte argentino en los años sesenta* (Buenos Aires: Paidós, 2001), pp. 372–73.

25. Cf. D. Garcia and G. Lovink, "The ABC of Tactical Media," www.waag.org/tmn/abc.html. Also see the wide variety of projects that have been discussed in the "Next 5 Minutes" festivals, www.n5m.org. Today, Indymedia is considered (by some) as the major expression of tactical media.
26. Cf. "Friday June 18th 1999: Confronting Capital and Smashing the State!" in *Do or Die* 8, London, online at www.eco-action.org/dod/no8/j18.html.
27. See www.corporatewatch.org.uk/magazine/issue8/cw8glob6.html.

7

LIAR'S POKER

REPRESENTATION OF POLITICS / POLITICS OF REPRESENTATION

Basically, what I have to say here is simple: when people talk about politics in an artistic frame, they're lying. Indeed, the lies they tell are often painfully obvious, and worse is the moment when you realize that some will go forever unchallenged and take on, not the semblance of truth, but the reliability of convention. In a period like ours when the relationship to politics is one of the legitimating arguments for the very existence of public art, the tissue of lies that surrounds you when entering a museum can become so dense that it's like falling into an ancient cellar full of spider webs, and choking on them as you struggle to breathe. Now, the mere mention of this reality will make even my friends and allies in the artistic establishment rather nervous; but it is a reality nonetheless. And like most of the political realities in our democratic age, it has directly to do with the question of representation.

PICTURE POLITICS

Does anyone doubt there exists a politics of representation? Such people have clearly not looked at the television during a political campaign. But worse, they have not looked at social movements. They have not witnessed the endless capacity of people who do not occupy positions of elite power, and who do not enjoy direct access to major media, to project their messages nonetheless, by means of signs, images and gestures. Nor have they realized how effectively artists can work in such "outside" contexts: one need only think of Gran Fury, amidst the New York Aids activism of the 1980s; of Ne Pas Plier, with the jobless people's movements in Paris in the 1990s; or of the many artists who have participated in recent counter-globalization demonstrations and campaigns. Artists can play a vital role in this kind of "picture politics."

At the same time, it is easy for artists to heed the injunction of the museum, the magazines and the market, which say: "Picture politics for me." Do a picture or a sculpture of politics, carry out the representation of political conflict, as in the installation piece by Thomas Hirschhorn, *Wirtschaftslandschaft Davos* ("Economic Landscape Davos"), shown at Kunsthaus Zürich when Hirschhorn won the prize for "Young Swiss Art" in 2001. This work uses model houses, toy soldiers, real barbed wire and other ready-made materials to represent the besieged Swiss valley where the world's most powerful people annually meet. Hirschhorn's style can be referenced to "dadaist collage," observes one critic; but his major source is "the practice of excluded people who know perfectly well how to get their messages across, by using whatever they find."[1] In this case the excluded people are those who confront the barbed wire at the World Economic Forum. And since counter-globalization has been a hot subject, representing them is a perfect way to become popular in a museum.

Hirschhorn goes further, though, because he turns a bit of ordinary life into a representation of politics, with his *Bataille Monument* in a Turkish quarter of Kassel. This life-sized library, snack bar and makeshift TV studio is a participatory project, whose effects in the neighborhood itself I won't presume to judge from a distance. What concerns me is the way he manages its relations to the artistic frame. On the "taxi stand" where visitors awaited to be ferried from the Documenta 11 to the site of the monument, Hirschhorn placed a quotation from the American artist, David Hammonds: "The art audience is the worst audience in the world. It's overly educated, it's conservative, it's out to criticize, not to understand and it never has any fun.... So I refuse to deal with that audience, and I'll play with the street audience. That audience is much more human, and their opinion is from the heart. They don't have any reason to play games, there's nothing gained or lost." Hirschhorn claims to have abandoned the framing structures of contemporary art, for a more authentically engaged social practice. But if that's the case, why the taxi, why the exposure of the site to visitors' eyes, which turns the social project into a representation? What kind of game is he playing?

In his case there are certainly things to be won—like the prize for Young Swiss Art, or the Marcel Duchamp prize for the promotion of French artists, awarded to Hirschhorn by the ADIAF association in the year 2000. The Duchamp prize is sponsored by Pricewaterhouse-Coopers, a transnational consulting company, specializing in mergers and acquisitions. Kunsthaus Zürich, where *Wirtschaftslandschaft Davos* was shown, is regularly funded by the Private Banking subsidiary of Crédit Suisse, which ranks 31st on *Fortune's* Global 500 list. Documenta 11 was sponsored by Volkswagen, Deutsche Telekom and Sparkassen-Finanzgruppe. Does all this sound familiar? In the contemporary art game, the picture of excluded people's politics is worth a lot to the included—including transnational corporations. Of course I'm aware that the prize commissions are independent, just like exhibition curators. Their independence supports the notion of an autonomous artistic sphere, separate from the economic nexus that sustains it. These kinds of separations, between abstract financial decisions and their substantive effects, are exactly what the protestors at the Davos meetings refuse. Hirschhorn, for his part, retains an obvious interest in the artistic frame he claims to leave behind. Yet he seems particularly uncomfortable there; and it's intriguing to see how he ups the symbolic stakes in the Davos piece, formulating a direct critique of transnational capitalism even as he is pursued and courted by the corporate-backed prize commissions.

How does picture politics work, when it is associated with a proper name and presented within the contemplative frame of the art institution? Invariably it produces statements like these: "I represent the people," or "I represent a social movement," or "I represent the excluded"—which are the classic lies of representative democracy, when it serves to conceal private interests.[2] Of course, this root fact makes myself, a self-styled "critic" writing in catalogues and magazines about the relations of art and politics, into one of the baldest liars of them all. And for some perverse reason I want to tell you how it's done.

RULES OF THE GAME

Liar's poker is easy to play. The deck is composed of kings and aces. One person draws, and names the card in his hand; the other judges if he's telling the truth. If you draw an ace, it's easy: you have no choice but to say it's an ace. If you draw a king, then the game begins: because you can always bluff. Each time you claim to hold an ace, the other player must look you in the eyes and decide if it's real. If he thinks it's not, he calls your bluff; and if he's right he wins a dollar, or ten, or a hundred, depending on how high you've set the stakes. If he's wrong, you win the same. And if he doesn't do a thing, he loses fifty cents, or five bucks, or fifty dollars, and the card goes back into the pack, so that no one ever knows if you were telling the truth.

For our purposes, the artist draws the cards, and the public calls the bluffs. Nowadays, of course, the artist often plays as a team with the curator or the critic; so those relations are never entirely certain. As for the cards, the ace is political reality, and its image in the museum is highly attractive. This gives the artist a great advantage: because to prove an ace is a bluff, you have to go out looking, whereas the public prefers to stay inside the museum. The artist, however, also has a great disadvantage, which is that the house—I mean the people who run the game, the founders, the funders, the boards and directors—actually can't stand aces, and if they think the artist really has one, they will never let him or her set foot inside the museum. So in both cases the artist has to bluff his way through, either claiming political engagement to live like a king inside the white cube, or hiding it to siphon off money, resources and publicity for use by a social movement. Occasionally, when the lie is too grotesque, the public will call the bluff; and then the artist has to give up some cultural capital. Even more rarely, it turns out that the artist is really involved in a social movement, in which case he or she is soon fated to disappear from the museum.

Now there's an obvious question: Why would anyone want to play such a game? In fact the question can be asked about anyone playing by the unbearable rules that hold in almost every social field today. These are the rules of inequality, exploitation, domination—those nasty realities we have to lie about in polite democratic society. When Pierre Bourdieu developed his theory of the semi-autonomous, rule-governed social fields, he first had to ask why people participate. He pointed to different forms of interest. Individuals can have a monetary interest in participating in a given field, they can do it to acquire *economic capital*. They can also have an interest in the relations to be formed with powerful people, so they play to acquire *social capital*. But in the highly professional world of art, even more than in most other fields, social capital is at least partially acquired through the accumulation of *cultural capital*, which can be conceived as the ability to produce, recombine and display the very specific types of signs, images and gestures which are most valued within a given field at a particular period. Accumulating cultural capital means mastering complex fetishes of meaning which have been constructed and transformed over time. Thus it becomes apparent that a powerful function of belief is at work. You must believe that these fetishes are really valuable, or "interesting." Bourdieu came to call this belief *illusio*, which he defines as "the fact of being invested, caught up in and by the game." "Being interested," he continues, "means ascribing a meaning to what happens in a given social game, accepting that its stakes are important and worthy of being pursued."³ In the game we are discussing, the fundamental interest (or illusion) is the attainment of autonomy: an historical ideal whose terms are open to endless struggle.⁴ There is a passion of this *illusio* without which it would be impossible to understand what happens in the artistic field today—in particular its lies, its bluffs, its representations.

Can the *illusio* that accounts for the very coherency of the field be transformed, gravitationally shifted, so that its prestigious objects—the signs, gestures and images—are reevaluated? Such a result could only come about through a shake-up in the system of positions occupied by specific players. This is what we are now witnessing. In the artistic game of liar's poker, certain players are increasing the stakes, and steering the conventional bluff of picture politics to the point where the contract that holds together the artist, the curator, the public and the house—that is to say, the museum as a social institution—finally breaks. When you can bluff your way to a very dramatic break, then there is the possibility of changing the field itself, of beginning to play a different game.

UPPING THE STAKES

Let's recall certain wagers that link the 1997 Documenta (dX) to the 2002 edition (D11). The former attempted to reknit the ties between poetics and politics, within a history considered on a world scale. Its major innovation—the 100 Days lecture program organized by Catherine David—was a Napoleonic conquest of neoliberal globalization as an object for artistic discourse. Perhaps the exhibition as a whole could have been criticized for using intellectuals and historical artists to represent a protagonism that the consensus of the European scene could not offer at that time. An essay in the catalogue by Masao Miyoshi, illustrated with a geopolitical map by the late Oyvind Fahlström, sums up the equation. Entitled "A Borderless World?," it gives a detailed account of the rise of the transnational corporation and the attendant changes in the hegemonic functions of culture. Miyoshi asks the key question: "Are the intellectuals of the world willing to participate in transnational corporatism and be its apologists?"⁵ But what no one said is how the world's living artists, critics and curators could convincingly answer, in the negative.

No one on the center stage, that is. But part of the dX bluff was to include a cutting edge, the so-called "new technologies." The Hybrid WorkSpace would be inhabited, among others, by artist-activists making their first uses of the Internet, for a ten-day worshop called [*über die grenze*]. I quote from an interview with Florian Schneider that appeared on the *sans-papiers* website founded by a French social movement shortly after the occupation of Saint-Bernard Church in Paris in 1996:

> Q: About the Documenta, here, you can talk about illegal people in a very famous art exhibition. I think it is not so easy to do such things in France. Do you think it's easier in Germany, or is there something special here, at the Documenta? You're talking about illegal people!...
>
> A: Yes, sure, we are also a little bit surprised. On one hand we obviously have a fool's license here, we can declare everything, we can also nearly practice everything. On Sunday, we opened a passport exchange office, and we asked people to give us their passport to pass it on people who need it much more, which are undocumented or so called illegal people. A policeman appeared, and he asked 'is this art or not? what are you going to do with the passports?' And we asked him for his passport. He refused to give us his passport, but he promised us to talk with his superiors about the action, and that was what we wanted to reach. So it seems that we could do everything we want. It's great and very funny, but in the same way, it makes me nervous a little bit, because there is even no reaction by the other side. That's the main problem in the art context. We decided to use the possibility to make politics here because it's very important at this moment to spread the campaign we started, and to spread the aims we have, spread them very widely.⁶

The participants of [*über die grenze*] broke the conventional contract with the art institution, by refusing to stop at the borders of representation. Taking literally the corporate rhetoric about freedom of movement under globalization, they used dX as a physical and virtual platform to spread a new campaign, indeed, a new form of self-organization: the social movement Kein Mensch ist illegal, which over the last five years has not ceased to grow and metamorphose, continually changing names, languages, spokespeople, participants, tactics... D11 recognized the importance of this autonomous, non-representational politics by inviting Florian Schneider to speak at the first of its "Platforms," held in April 2001 under the title "Democracy Unrealized." A year later, a No Border camp was organized by activists in protest against the Schengen Information System in Strasbourg, while D11 raked in the tourist crowds in Kassel.

Personally, I had entirely missed the Hybrid Work Space in 1997. But I did take part in the recent No Border camp with the conceptual group Bureau d'Etudes, distributing a cartographic work—or what you might just call a tract—entitled *Refuse the Biopolice*. One of the best encounters in Strasbourg was the Publix Theater Caravan, with a multimedia laboratory inside, a traveling café on top and a theater troupe performing anti-deportation interventions in public space. A week after the camp I found myself in Kassel, amazed to see a tremendous spectrum of precise and moving artworks, whose focus, in the majority of cases, was either oppression and imprisonment, or even more often, the contemporary border regime. The activist pretensions of an experimental group in 1997, and the direct action of a social movement today, seemed to be justified, extended, deepened by almost every piece in the immense exhibition.

By searching across the world, D11 found the artists to support the critique that had been formulated in the previous edition. After watching Amar Kanwar's video on the Indo-Pakistani conflict, including fascinating shots of the ritual closing of the militarized border between the two countries, I stepped out into the sunlight to discover none other than the Publix Theater bus, parked in front of the Fridericianum. To me it looked like a homecoming. But the next surprise was a police officer ordering the bus to leave, under the guidance of a Documenta security manager. The troupe chanted over their PA system, "Thank you, thank you to the German police for this beautiful performance, free speech is being silenced everywhere, thank you, thank you." And then someone walked up to the manager and the chief cop and handed them *Refuse the Biopolice*. Both proceeded instinctively to roll it up into the form of a military man's baton—as though artworks, in the hands of power, could only be a weapon and nothing more.[7]

PLAYING THE ACE

"Artistic freedom is a fundamental right. And we feel free to promote it," proclaims the Sparkassen-Finanzgruppe in the pages of the D11 catalogue. You wonder how they feel about all the artists participating in the current round of social struggles. Take one example: Las Agencias, a group which came together shortly before a week-long conference and workshop in October 2000 at the Museum of Contemporary Art in Barcelona, with an impressive list of picture-politicians (®™ark, Reclaim the Streets, Kein Mensch ist illegal, Ne pas plier, Communication Guerrilla, London Indymedia...). The program was called "On Direct Action as One of the Fine Arts." Held at the public's insistence outside the museum, in an anarchist union hall, it was a great success. Work continued for months thereafter on subjects like free money, activist fashion design, the practical use of pictorial shields, and a traveling Show Bus to bring culture to the people. Then, on the day of huge demonstrations organized against the World Bank in March 2002—when 500,000 people took to the streets of Barcelona—the local police came to raid the bar of the MacBa, used by Las Agencias. And in the weeks after this event, the Show Bus was attacked and destroyed in broad daylight—undoubtedly by undercover police. It goes without saying that the breaking point had been reached: Las Agencias could no longer be funded by the museum. Pursuing their *détournement* of consumer ideologies, the group started a new campaign around the theme Yo Mango, a slogan referring to a trendy fashion brand—but which also translates as "Just Nick It." Yo Mango practices redistributive shoplifting, in the spirit of thousands of unemployed Argentineans whom the international banking system left with no other choice than to steal their dinner, ransacking transnational supermarket chains. Is this artistic freedom? Yo Mango has become a social movement, crossing the border of representation. But from time to time—to the rage of some former members—they still exhibit in museums. Meanwhile, the MacBa continues its inquiry into the relations of art and politics, more legitimately and subversively than ever.

Political involvement is popular in art right now, and for good reasons. How do art professionals maneuver in this environment, between pressures from the public on the one hand, and from the financial backers of the institutional "house" on the other? What kind of game do they play? Bourdieu has this to say about moments of aesthetic transformation: "Revolutions in art result from the transformation of the power relations constituting the space of artistic positions, a transformation which itself is rendered possible by a coincidence between the subversive intentions of a fraction of the producers and the expectations of a fraction of their public."[8] We have seen this type of situation emerging over the past few years, as the globalized, flexibilized economy shakes up the hierarchy of social positions, rendering new alliances imaginable. And it is clear that some art professionals are playing the beginnings of a transformative game. But it would be naive to think that others do not see these situations unfolding. The art of maintaining social balances through the management of cultural trends has long been developed by the European social democracies, and is being taken over by the privatized institutions.[9] In other words, we must suppose that a fraction of those in power seek to manipulate the public, by instrumentalizing the cultural producers who play their tricks for them.

Our problem is to account for the strange duplicity of art institutions. Consider Documenta again. Why did the people who run what used to be the ideological set-piece of "Western art," created during the Cold War less than fifty kilometers from the East German border, with the transparent aim of exalting the abstractions of subjective freedom in the face of socialist realism, suddenly decide to pick as curator, first a French woman with a lingering Marxist mentality and a strong interest in Brazil, then a Nigerian man with an intense investment in postcolonial theory and historiography? The only realistic answer I can find is that those who make the decisions saw that the first post-89 edition, curated in 1992 by Jan Hoet—a chic, friendly and mildly patronizing art-world type with "good taste" and a willingness to have fun without rocking the boat—was perceived within the artistic field as a gigantic flop. Just more of the same, looking paunchy and overprivileged. How then could Documenta remain at the cutting edge? If the Cold War was over, shouldn't the flagship "Western" exhibition now somehow engage with globalization? Did that not first entail finding out something about what globalization is (Catherine David's highly analytic show), then diving right into and producing its multicultural legitimacy by actually exhibiting living artists from outside Germany, England, Italy, France and the USA—people who had never made the cover of *Flash Art* or *Artforum*?

The institutional "house" now seeks its interest in a complex game, which alone can reconcile the economic nexus it provides with the cultural capital its seeks among the more radical fractions of the artistic field. It must ask its cultural producers for the ace of politics, while proving all the while (with the help of the police, if need be) that this ace is merely a bluff, that it is really a king (the sovereign power of illusion in representative democracies). And yet it is through this double game that new symbolic possibilities for conceiving and shaping the ways we live—what Nietzsche might have called "the transvaluation of all values"—can be distributed on the scale that an exhibition like Documenta offers. The Nietzschean dance happens not in some glorious void of the contemplative intellect, but in the real world. You have people whose genuine radicality is also a beckoning chance for career advancement, being instrumentalized by others who want added legitimacy for a globalized society facing a groundswell of critique. And the instability of the game—the depth of its gaping contradictions—has rarely been so great as today, while the corporate rhetoric unravels and everyone must face the reality of their positions in the contemporary economy, with its proliferating borders.

An example of how these contradictions unfold was the ad hoc "Platform 6," called for 24 hours on the lawn in front of the Fridericianum, by No Border again, in collaboration with Rom people facing expulsion from Germany. This time the obvious parallels between the activist demands and the artistic arguments developed within the show itself helped overcome the resistance of the security team. Just imagine, for a moment, the different kinds of cultural capital that suddenly appeared on the table: "Okwui Enwzor, the Documenta's artistic director, called from New York. The curator Ute Meta Bauer and other artists and collaborators intervened. Thomas Hirschorn and some artists and employees of the exhibition had passionate discussions about the hierarchy and the security system. A pretty intense night, all in all."[1]

The institutional struggle becomes visible at unexpected moments like these, when everyone involved must take a public stand on the real value of the symbolic cards they are playing.

BEYOND REPRESENTATION

These observations are pragmatic, based on personal experience. The truth is that the strategies of liar's poker are inevitable today, as cultural institutions both public and private try to mediate between the logic of profit and prestige and the desire for alternative valuations. But that can be put more bluntly: in the age of corporate patronage and the neoliberal state, art is becoming a field of extreme hypocrisy.[11] And so it directly reflects the crisis of the representative democracies. The temptation is then to cease playing the game (the anarchist solution), or to simply exploit the museum's resources for other ends ("radical media pragmatism"). Both positions are justified, from the activist point of view. But there are disadvantages to leaving entire sectors of society to rot, as each new swing to the neo-authoritarian right is there to prove. The most interesting question within the artistic field then becomes: How to play the exhibition game in such a way that something real can actually be won?

The very notion of cultural capital shows how domination operates through forms that need no longer have anything to do with rarity or accumulation. And the beauty of art in its turn away from the object is precisely that you can give it away: *Dinero Gratis*, as some friends of the Yo Mango group like to say. Art today is one of the few fields open to experimentation with the technologies, habits and hierarchies of symbolic exchange, fundamental to a media-driven society. But these experiments can only take on a transformative power in the open, evolving context of a social movement, outside the cliques and clienteles of the artistic game. Which is why even the work of someone as outwardly radical as Thomas Hirschhorn appears so dubious. How can anyone be sure of its success, when the reception is dominated by his proper name?

The rising fortunes of interventionist art, the multiplication of exhibitions devoted to sociopolitical issues and activist campaigns, are proof enough that something political is at stake in the artistic field. And the stakes keep rising, as artists, curators and critics vie for radicality, relevancy, effectiveness and meaning. But one must constantly question what kind of currency we'll get when the chips are cashed in. The only way to go beyond the small change of individual prestige on the institutional market is to radically reverse the valuations effected by the critical gaze. And this requires an effort from a great many players of the game: a transformation of the very definition of cultural capital, a shift in the *illusio* of the artistic field. What is ultimately at stake is the very definition of autonomy, which can no longer be established in the sphere of representation alone.

Right now, the greatest symbolic innovations are taking place in self-organization processes unfolding outside the artistic frame. And it is from the reference to such outside realms that the more concentrated, composed and self-reflective works in the museum take their meaning. The only way not to impoverish those works, or to reduce them to pure hypocrisy, is to let our highest admiration go out to the artists who call their own bluffs—and dissolve, at the crisis points, into the vortex of a social movement.

Notes

1. "Thomas Hirschhorn, Wirtschaftlandschaft Davos," by Patrick Schaefer, in *L'art en jeu*, online magazine: www.art-en-jeu.ch/expositions/hirschhorn.html.
2. Cf. Bureau d'Etudes, "Cadavre de l'autonomie artistique," in *Autonomie artistique et société de communication* 1 (Paris, 2002).
3. Pierre Bourdieu, *Réponses* (Paris: Seuil, 1992), p. 92.
4. Bourdieu devoted an entire work to the historical process whereby the ideal of autonomy was constituted in France, and to the present field of struggle it opens up: *Les Règles de l'art* (Paris: Seuil, 1992).
5. *Politics/Poetics, Documenta X—The Book* (Ostfildern: Cantz, 1997), p. 193.
6. At www.bok.net/pajol/international/kassel/florian.en.html.

7. For general info on the Publix Theater group, see http://en.wikipedia.org/wiki/Publixtheatre_Caravan. For an account of these particular events, see Gini Müller, "Traversal or Terror? Moving Images of the Publix Theater Caravan," at www.republicart.net/disc/hybridresistance/mueller01_en.htm. I am told, by way of excuse for the police action, that an Israeli delegation, visiting that day, had asked for maximum security. But of course this precise request is part of the worldwide security and border system.
8. Bourdieu, *Réponses*, p. 81. For a full development, see the last chapter of *Homo Academicus* (Paris: Minuit, 1984).
9. In Europe, the most relevant model of this takeover process is Third-Way cultural policy in Britain; see former culture minister Chris Smith's book, *Creative Britain*, and the discussions in Julian Stallabrass, *High Art Lite* (London: Verso, 1999), chaps. 6 and 7.
10. See "Traversal or Terror?" op. cit.
11. Gregory Sholette offers a precise observation about the "fool's license" given to a certain kind of critical art: "What has been revealed by the institutional critique is one persistent and disturbing fact: many cultural institutions are led by the private interests and personal tastes of an invisible elite, rather than by their stated philanthropic and educational mission. Yet while the institutional critique has directly focused significant attention on this cultural contradiction for the past thirty years, it now appears to provide a degree of closure by reinforcing the notion that the museum offers an uncompromising democratic zone for engaging in civic dialogue." "Fidelity, Betrayal, Autonomy: In and Beyond the Post-Cold War Art Museum," *Third Text*, Summer 2002.

8

POLICY OF TRUTH

CRITICAL ART IN CORPORATE INSTITUTIONS

The Generali Foundation, an entirely corporate-funded museum in Vienna, has acquired an enviable reputation for staging ambitious, culturally critical exhibitions. Paying homage to the conceptual art and institutional critique of the 1960s, '70s, and '80s, its curatorial policy has established important threads of historical continuity across several generations of artists whose importance was overlooked during much of the 1990s. At a time when the art market had relegated the politics of representation to the back burner, one-person exhibitions on Adrian Piper, Martha Rosler, and Andrea Fraser made Generali an important and proactive site for the production of feminist cultural discourse.

The recent Generali exhibition, *Geography and the Politics of Mobility*, was a timely advance on these individual retrospectives. This show, curated by video artist Ursula Biemann, brought together a group of contemporary artists exploring state-corporate power, globalised labour relations, and migration. Its tacit object of critique was the capitalist system and the types of political relations it brings into being.

This might seem surprising for a cultural institution whose sole patron is one of the largest insurance companies in the world. Equally, participating in the show could pose complex political problems for the corporate-critical artists working under its aegis. Brian Holmes is an affiliate of exhibitors Bureau d'Ètudes (see *Mute* 24), a contributor to the exhibition catalogue, and—in an article in Springerin magazine—one of the few to publicly take the show's bull of an issue by the horns. *Mute* asked him to discuss his rationale for taking part, and to elaborate on his statement that a policy of straight-talking is the only genuinely disruptive move.

The mapping of contemporary capitalism, undertaken in different ways by thousands of involved intellectuals over the last decade, has made certain realities clear. That the basis of life insurance is death, for one thing. Corporate funds investing the savings of the comfort classes are major players in the worldwide game of financial speculation, whose results are a deadly imbalance of over- and underdevelopment, acceleration and decay, glut and starvation. Bankers and insurance people keep their hands perfectly clean. They are also great art patrons. Would you like to take their dirty money home with you?

Once again the question was looking me in the face. Ursula Biemann had organised what seemed like a useful and intelligent exhibition under the title *Geography and the Politics of Mobility*, with groups like Makrolab, Multiplicity, Raqs Media Collective and Bureau d'Ètudes. I was interested in the project, and she invited me to write a catalogue text. It described the emergence of an activist "art at large," realizing some of the original goals of conceptual art by achieving autonomous distribution at increasingly large scales. It also looked at the residual relations to specialized exhibition spaces: "For the tactical media underground in Europe, art shows offer useful research deadlines, a chance to share ideas and critiques, at best some production money— and at worst, a damaging distraction. The revenge of the concept has been to finally create parallel and alternative circuits of experimentation, production, distribution, use and interpretation. To be sure, these circuits are hardly consolidated—but the best way to do so is to maintain other urgencies, which cannot be treated within any of the specialised subsystems."

The position was fairly clear. But the actual site of the show in question—the Generali Foundation in Vienna—was still part of the game. And we all know that uncomfortable feeling. At whatever distance you place the operations of a foundation from the financial holding behind it, the connection through the proper name is complete. These kinds of foundations are unbearable—whether it's a place like Cartier in Paris, which blatantly wields cultural power for corporate ends, or Generali, which has picked institutional critique as their brand of hypocritical theory.

I had a chance to speak in Vienna about a month before the opening, within the prestigious new MuseumQuartier, which itself looks something like a banking complex for pictures. I'd already funneled Generali's cash for the text to a Bureau d'Ètudes war-chest for future projects (the art-world equivalent of Geert Lovink's 'radical media pragmatism'). But the prospect of a talk raised a more important question: how to maintain the "other urgencies" in a situation of public debate? We had to back up the explicitly anti-capitalist maps of Bureau d'Ètudes with some concrete work in Vienna that would overflow the frames of the art system.

A critical position should go to the heart of the actual relation. People who theorize anti-capitalism are invited to a foundation emanating from a major European life-insurance company. What are they likely to do in practice, besides diverting the production money? What interests me are the ways that power relations get translated symbolically—that is, the struggle over cultural capital. In the last few years it has been intensifying, all over Europe. Now it seemed possible to go one step further, by laying the cards out on the table. So I wrote a description of the game, "Liar's Poker," (published in *Springerin* 1/03, and reprinted in this volume).

"Liar's Poker" describes a fundamental hypocrisy that plagues the capitalist democracies. It's a fact which is itself a provocation. Still there's nothing more interesting than trying to produce the truth in public. And for that you have to create the opportunities. Vienna is the home of Public Netbase. It's the kind of institution that has marked out a space of debate by constant and careful struggle with various levels of the state, essentially over questions of access and legitimacy. Not by chance have they worked for years on the use of networked tools for political experimentation. Nor by chance were they forced out of the MuseumsQuartier at the moment of its renovation. It seemed like a place for a deeper discussion of the mapping project, one that could involve a wider variety of actors. We decided to hold a parallel debate there, a day before the lecture program at the Generali. It turned into a parallel exhibition and distribution point for the Bureau d'Ètudes' publications.

One of the things a critic can do is to look for confrontations, where the stakes in an argument become explicit. The two exhibitions in Vienna were a successful experiment in that direction. They showed that when you work with capable local people, you can organise a public thinking process, one that cuts through different levels of engagement. The discussion at Netbase went a long way, because it was obvious we were making an effort to find out what words mean. But for that to happen in a hypocritical society, some kind of conflict has to be visible. And I think it's important to press your position at every level. There are so many good people caught up in art, for so many good reasons. It's just too late in the day to hang around gnawing the bones of institutional critique.

To get started you have to name things, talk straight for a change. Proper names are the signatures of property, which on the level of finance has now become flagrant abuse. In the contemporary situation, cultural capital has become dirty money you can't reinvest: it clings to your signature. Corporate power has to be challenged linguistically, by hundreds of thousands of ordinary intellectuals, in the street and in all the public spaces and media. If you can steal their megaphones, use 'em for a day. But maybe it's better to think about finding a few of your own for the long run. Just to insure a more autonomous future.

[Published in *Mute* 26, 4/7/2003]

9

ARTISTIC AUTONOMY & THE COMMUNICATION SOCIETY

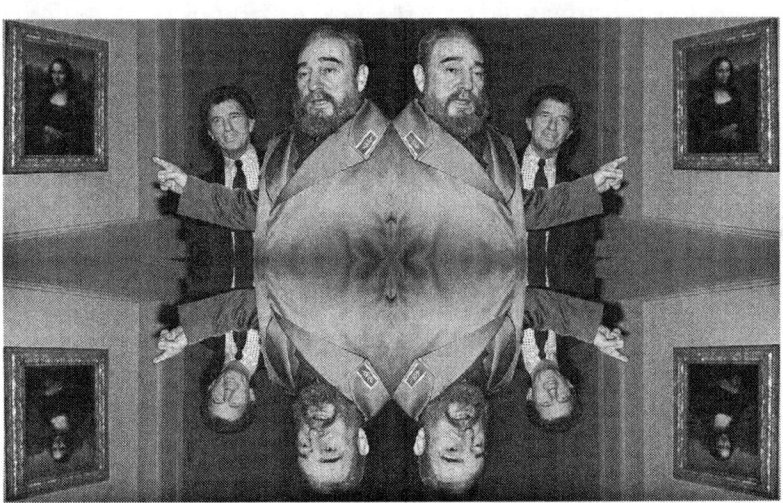

The period in which we are living has seen a sweeping change in the organization and fundamental mission of the aesthetic institutions (museums, schools, publishing houses, forms of patronage, etc.), a change driven ahead by the transformation of society on the business model. One characteristic of this accelerated change has been to make artistic and cultural production both into a major field for capital valorization, and into an important means of controlling and channeling the aspirations of populations, partially replacing the disciplinary frameworks of the mass-production society. In this context, there is need for a broad and intense debate about the means, results and ends of artistic practice, independent from the categories established by the market and the state. This was one of the motivations for an initial, collaborative publication in French, coordinated by Bureau d'Ètudes and myself, under the title *Autonomie artistique—et société de communication*. Here I will pursue some specific aspects of that same debate.

Why talk about autonomy when the major thrust of experimental art in the 1960s and 70s was to undermine the autonomous work? This is the question that always arises when you speak with those for whom the academic discourses of the 1950s still seem to matter. Indeed, the university careers to be made by refuting Greenburg, by deconstructing the harmonious totality of the white male Kantian subject, by critiquing the closure of the artistic frame, are seemingly infinite. And the same holds for the description of the paradoxes that invariably arise when mechanically reproduced works or recorded slices of everyday life are presented in the auratic, singularizing spaces of the museum. But one sometimes wonders if the members of the art establishment, while seemingly obsessed with these transgressions of a very old status quo, are in fact not afraid to draw the most basic conclusions from their own ideas. For if you truly abandon the notion that an object, by its distinction from all others, can serve as a mirror for an equally unique and independent subject, then the issue of autonomy becomes a deep existential problem. Because for those without a substitute identity, for those without a passionate belief in their blackness, their whiteness, their Jewishness, their Muslimness, their Communistness, their Britishness or whatever, the condition of existence in the communication society—that is, the awareness that one's own mental processes are intimately traversed or even determined by a ceaseless flux of mediated images and signs—is at first deeply anguishing, then ultimately anesthetizing, as basic structures of the ego dissolve and the postmodern "waning of affect" sets in.[2] We always work beneath the pall of this postmodern anesthetic.

No doubt there are thousands of very exciting ways to make artworks where the question of autonomy is not at issue. But there is some doubt as to whether any of these ways of art-making could be called political. Does politics, in the democratic sense at least, not presuppose that one is somehow able to make a free decision? That one is not blindly driven by a determining, heteronomous force? What does it mean to make an artistic decision? And what happens when that decision is collective? How can the sensible world—that is, the world composed by the senses, the intellect and the imagination—be reshaped according to what the artist François Deck would call a "strategy of freedom"?

The stakes of autonomy are revealed by the etymology of the word, as pointed out by the psychoanalyst and political philosopher Cornelius Castoriadis. *Autos* means self, and *nomos* means law. Autonomy means giving yourself your own law.[3] But men and women are social beings; we only exist as "ourselves" through the language of the other, through the sensations of the other; and what is more, this shared language, these transiting sensations, are bound up in the uncertainty of memory and forgetting, the incompleteness of perception, the willfulness of imagination, the specific materiality of expression. Thus, the attempt to give oneself one's own law becomes a collective adventure, as well as a cultural and artistic one.[4] For it is the very essence of clear consciousness to recognize that we human beings are full of obscurity, of unresolved personal and historical passions, of half-understood images and enticing forms that we constantly exchange with one another, generating the majority of our motivations and behaviors in the process, so that the act of giving ourselves our own laws becomes something quite complex, something experimental and experiential, which can never be resolved once and for all, but only cared for and coaxed along in manifold ways, among which we find the arts—those supreme expressions of sensation, intellect and imagination. Indeed, it is exactly with respect to art and its reception, or better, its uses, that freedom appears fundamentally as a open strategy among the multitudes, because the dynamic of expression and use can never be directed by the one—that is, by any sovereign instance of decision. And in this way, collective autonomy becomes a question both of individual or small-group artistic production, and of the large-scale cultural policy that conditions its reception and uses.

My belief is that you can only have a real democracy when a societal concern with the production of the sensible is maintained at the level of a forever unresolved but constantly open and intensely debated question. This is why I like to work with François Deck, because he has developed a method, a kind of artistic trick—the "question banks" and associated procedures—that allows him to explicitly bring the sensible world into collective questioning. What we really need is to spend a lot more time asking each other whether our cultural fictions—our architecture and images, our hierarchies and ambitions and ideas and narratives—are any good for us, whether they can be used in an interesting way, what kind of subjectivity they produce, what kind of society they elicit. But to do that effectively, we also need to invent new fictions, to shake up the instituted imaginary with what Castoriadis calls the "radical" or "instituting" imaginary.[5] Only by actively imagining different possible realities can we engage in the operations of desymbolization and resymbolization, or in what Bureau d'Études calls "the deconstruction and reconstruction of complex machines"—taking the notion of machines in the strong sense, whereby it denotes the symbolic, technological and human assemblages that configure ourselves and our societies, and make them work in the specific ways they do.[6]

Art can offer a chance for society to collectively reflect on the imaginary figures it depends upon for its very consistency, its self-understanding. But this is exactly where our societies are failing, and failing miserably, as a result of the way artistic invention and display has been instituted as a central economic function over the last twenty years. We are looking at an extreme limitation on the varieties and qualities of self-reflection. To indicate the extent of this disaster, and the degree to which it calls for a reinvention of artistic autonomy, I will take two examples. One is a programmatic sentence from the former French culture minister, Jack Lang. And the other is the concrete reality of a major British museum. These examples will give a fairly precise idea of what I mean by the communication society, and why it's necessary to conceive artistic autonomy against the background of the really existing machines of communication.

Jack Lang is one of the great socialist managers of people's minds, one of the major architects of artistic creation. Imagine him as he appears in a photo which can be found on the Internet, standing in front of the Mona Lisa with one of his few living peers, Fidel Castro.7 In 1983, the year French socialism abandoned its collectivist utopia —that is to say, its real political program, the one it was democratically elected for—in the face of the so-called economic crisis, Lang came out with this slogan: "Culture is the poets, plus electricity." *La culture, c'est les poètes, plus l'électricité.* Extraordinary man, to say such a thing! "This kind of mesmerism is a constant in his conception of art," remarks a French observer. For Lang, "culture is an economic weapon because it can change mentalities, and because the crisis is not just economic, but also a crisis of the mind. The power of creativity is to elicit agitation, movement, to transform energy into labor."8

A lot of interesting ideas have been developed in the wake of the Italian Autonomia movement about the liberating potential of creative work, or what is called immaterial labor.9 But Jack Lang, like Chris Smith in Britain, is the state's great visionary of immaterial labor. And the state seeks only one thing: to functionalize creative work, to manage it, to give it a productive discipline. In the mid-1980s, Lang's culture ministry created an elaborate series of state-run institutions which aimed to modernize the artistic genres, to make them a flourishing, productive and prestigious part of a mixed economy with a "cultural exception." For Chris Smith, who came a decade later, the idea was literally to map out our sensations from above, to establish a "Creative Industries Mapping Document" that would productively channel people's aspirations into a thousand variations on the advertising industry.10 The cultural exception becomes the productive rule. Thus New Labour in Great Britain, more than any other European government, made a concerted attempt in the late 1990s to codify and professionalize the myriad of new behaviors which had emerged from the meeting of alienated urban youth and the new technologies for the creation and transmission of signs, sounds and images. The irony is that this kind of socialist central planning of the spirit reaches back to another would-be architect of humanity: Lenin, at the Congress of Soviets in 1920, who said: "Communism is soviet power, plus the electrification of the entire country." But which proved stronger: the workers' councils (soviets) or the programs of forced industrialization? And which do you think will prove stronger today: poetry or electricity?

The Tate Modern is a living allegory of these histories. It is a former electric power plant, a pure product of the meeting between the bureaucratic state and capitalist industry. This was a place for discipline, for the total control of a labor force. If you consider it architectonically, from the viewpoint of the volumes and the monumental order of the spaces, it looks like nothing so much as a mausoleum, a worker's tomb, which the party cadres of New Labour have turned into a tourist attraction, a crystal palace of globalization. It can be illuminated, decorated with blue neon light, electrified in its turn: so the tomb of the working class is made into a glittering artwork. Poetry meets electricity. And the Tate Modern also has a constructivist, Tatlinesque bridge that connects it directly to the heart of the City, as a public service for the bankers and traders of the financial district. It's important to admit what this kind of neoliberal institution is built on. The corporate sponsors of the Tate museums (both modern and classical) are at the heart, not just of British, but of Imperial capital: among them are Barclay's plc, Europe's largest institutional investor; Lloyds, the world's largest insurance company; British Telecom, one of the backbones of the communication society, a top advertiser and now the great British art patron; and BP, British Petroleum, rebranded "Beyond Petroleum," using art along with all the other forms of advertising to plant the sunflower seeds of an arcadian future in your oil-guzzling imagination. For corporations like these, creating belief, manipulating desire, and maintaining the political anesthesia of public life is the most important production.[11] And these companies now actively use the world of art, they make museums into private universities, like Bloomberg's holding seminars for its executives on Level 7, as a way to stimulate their energy, their experimental faculties, their virtuosity in the manipulation of abstract figures.[12] Of course this is all part of what is now the very well-known story of the privatization of culture from the Reagan and Thatcher era onward[13]—but it is equally coherent with the Third-Way strategies of workfare, which include the use of education and culture for the total mobilization of all the valuable, productive elements of the population.[14] And in this sense, far more so than in the days of the Situationists, art is the ultimate commodity, the one that sells all the rest. Because it mobilizes you, it plugs you into a transnational communications loop, it gets you to adhere, to commit, to do your part, to play your role, to burn the midnight oil, it makes you part of a dynamic society. A society whose imaginary of consumption/accumulation leads directly to the current wars in the Middle East.

What kind of attitude to take, when you know how tightly an institution like the Tate is integrated to what Bureau d'Ètudes has identified as the financial core of transnational state capitalism?[15] One thing is sure: the old strategy of forming a collective as a way to get into the museum has become absurd. That much has been proved by the submissive posturing of a group like Etoy, which endlessly reiterates the forms of corporate organization, from head-hunting rituals all the way down to the display of self-infantilization.[16] The collaborative art of Etoy only restates the painfully obvious: that the values of transnational state capitalism have permeated the art world, not only through the commodity form, but also, and even primarily, through the artists' adoption of managerial techniques and branded subjectivities. The current explosion of cleverly conceived "artists' collectives" thrusting themselves onto the institutional market is sorry testimony to this profound and unquestioning mimesis of the values projected from the consulting firms and human-resources departments. It is in this sense that contemporary capitalism has successfully absorbed the artistic critique of the 1960s, transforming it into the networked discipline of what Luc Boltanski and Eve Chiapello call "neo-management"—or into the subjective opportunism of what I call "the flexible personality."[17]

One response to all of this is—exit. Over the last ten years it has been increasingly possible to shift artistic work away from saleable objects, and outside the normative framework, into marginal realms of opposition whose consistency and sustainability over time becomes the key issue. A clear example can be found in the role of artists in sparking the counter-globalization protests, such as the "Carnival Against Capital" held in the City of London on June 18, 1999, and all the "Global Days of Action" that preceded and followed. Such experimental practices have benefited enormously from access to a cheap and relatively uncontrolled communication and distribution system, the Internet. Which is still a matter of poetry and electricity, but at the same time, quite another cup of tea. A deepening consciousness of personal stakes in the contemporary economy has more recently led young and not-so-young artists and theorists to participate in the self-organization of flexible workers, giving rise to a new kind of urban event, the Mayday parades, organized first in Milan, then in Barcelona.[18] In France, direct attacks from the right-wing government and the employers' organization have resulted in the struggle of the part-time theater and audiovisual workers to defend a special unemployment regime that helped shield them from the conditions of flexible labor, and so allowed them to practice their art outside the conditions dictated by the market. This struggle has directly identified the role of the dominant communications media in imposing a majority culture. On Saturday October 18, 2003, a group of part-time performers broke into a prime-time broadcast called "Star Academy." They seized the microphone to announce the demands of the movement and unfurled a banner reading: "Shut off your TVs." It was not an isolated event: innumerable broadcasts, ministerial speeches and film sets have been interrupted. Just a week before the Star Academy action, a networked movement had arisen to deface the advertisements that pollute the public space of the metro. Thousands of ads were destroyed over a period of a several months. These insurgencies constitute a live reflection on our collective fictions, on the instituted imaginary of the current neoliberal system.[19] And such symbolic violence, practiced collectively in the open air and raised to a level of engaged reflection on what we want our society to become, is a more interesting collaboration than anything I see in the museums. If we want to regain any chance at living in a democracy, we must make the production of the collective imaginary into an issue, by derailing or deconstructing certain communications machines, while building others and adapting the existing ones to meet new needs.

Shall we then abandon the museums? My position is that they can be occupied like any other distribution mechanism within the communication society-and should be occupied, to generate decisive conflict over the kind of society they help produce. But there is another, more challenging question: shall we abandon the historical practice of experimental art, as it emerged from its last metamorphosis in the period around 1968? Is the post-studio art of attitude and behavior fatally involved with the motivational strategies of neo-management, completely permeated with the opportunism and individualism of the flexible personality? One could draw such conclusions by observing the uses made of the "artistic critique" of the 1960s and 70s, as Boltanski and Chiapello do in *The New Spirit of Capitalism*. The imaginary of rebellion and liberation, the quest for individual authenticity, the ideal of self-management, the anti-hierarchical social form of the network/rhizome, all have been appropriated as rhetorical and organizational devices that respond to broad aspirations of emancipation, but deliberately channel those aspirations so as to reinstate exploitation and alienation under another guise. We can see the formula at work in communication machines like the Tate Modern, where the aesthetic populism of spectacular drifting on the ground floor combines with high-powered elite initiation on "Level 7," in a manner reminiscent of the double vulgo/culto reading offered in the Baroque spectacles as described by José Antonio Maravall.[20] Like the Baroque, the "guided culture" of twenty-first century hypermedia develops lavish and highly coordinated architectural environments and urban decors as manipulative devices offering various levels of participation, in the attempt to bind society into the appearance of a coherent and pleasurable whole, while at the same time reasserting the prerogatives of a ruling elite whose positions are threatened by the tremendous mobility and dynamism of the preceding period. The social institution of the imaginary operates simultaneously as a seductive capture device for popular desire, and as a productive discipline for the mid-ranking "symbolic analysts" (or "creative class") whose job it is to stimulate our interest, attention, passions—that is, to exercise the contemporary function of control, through the modulation of subjective energies.[21] Little wonder that museums like the Tate have attracted such attention from the highest managerial strata of what Félix Guattari used to call "integrated world capitalism."

Castoriadis sees a central role for the imaginary in the political project of autonomy, whereby a society attempts to give itself its own laws, and ultimately something like its own *habitus*, its own way of inhabiting the institutional structures. Conversely, he sees alienation as the result of an imaginary that cannot be reflected or reelaborated by those whose attitudes and behavior it conditions: "The essence of heteronomy at the individual level—or of alienation, in the general sense of the term—is domination by an imaginary which has become autonomous and has taken over the function of defining, for the subject, both reality and personal desire."[22] Here we rediscover the deeper meaning of the critique of the autonomous artwork developed in the sixties and the seventies. But today that critique must be turned to the full range of aesthetic institutions operating within spectacular society. How to destroy or surpass the central value placed on the economic within the imaginary institutions of the globalizing societies? To suggest the power of radical artistic practice to dissolve certain institutional forms, and to encourage the creation of others, I'd like to close with a reference to a group of artists from another epoch, close to the present and yet fundamentally different, who were not necessarily seeking to exit the museum, nor even the communication society, but who created a theatrical and conceptual fiction in a bid to reflexively transform the authoritarian state—which in their view had appropriated and distorted the avant-garde artistic tradition. I refer to the Slovene art group NSK, or Neue Slowenische Kunst, and particularly to their project, *The State in Time*. Its premises are described like this:

> In the year 1991 NSK has been re-defined from an Organization to a State. A state in time, a state without territory and national borders, a sort of "spiritual, virtual state." It has issued an original NSK passport and everybody can become its holder and therefore a citizen of the NSK State. The Passport can be used creatively, also as an official travel document, naturally with a certain hazard to its owner.... The NSK state denies... the categories of fixed territory, the principle of national borders, and advocates the law of transnationality. Besides NSK members the beneficiaries of the right to citizenship are thousands all over the world, people of different religions, races, nationalities, sexes and beliefs. The right to citizenship is acquired through ownership of the passport.[23]

Why did NSK create this strange conceptual machine, *The State in Time*? One reason was to assert the subjective consistency and sustainability of a group of people who effectively choose their own laws, who shape themselves and their society. This attempt to imagine the forms of autonomy was decisively important for NSK, as the Yugoslav federal state collapsed, and a new, but also unsatisfying—and potentially fascist—national state was born. But there is another level to this reflexive act, to this artistic transformation of the political imaginary. Because it is not so easy to create one's own laws. One only does so in the shadow of far larger organizations, really existing institutions, which can alienate your ideas and sensations, which can prey parasitically upon your deepest aspirations. And so the social forms of alienation must be exorcized, made to give back what they have captured, to release what they have appropriated and distorted. In the case of NSK, this alienating force was nothing less than the bureaucratic, disciplinary state, which in Yugoslavia bore the double heritage of Nazism and Stalinism. Both of these, in their view, had enduring consequences for artistic autonomy. As they write:

> Modern art has not yet overcome the conflict brought about by the rapid and efficient assimilation of historical avant-garde movements in the systems of totalitarian states.... [NSK] revives the trauma of avant-garde movements by identifying with it.... The most important and at the same time traumatic dimension of avant-garde movements is that they operate and create within a collective.... The question of collectivism, i.e. the question of how to organize communication and enable the coexistence of various autonomous individuals in a community, can be solved in two different ways. Modern states continue to be preoccupied with the question of how to collectivize and socialize the individual, whereas avant-garde movements tried to solve the question of how to individualize the collective. Avant-garde movements tried to develop autonomous social organisms in which the characteristics, needs and values of individualism, which cannot be comprised in the systems of a formal state, could be freely developed and defined. The collectivism of avant-garde movements had an experimental value. With the collapse of the avant-garde movements, social constructive views in art fell into disgrace, which caused the social escapism of orthodox modernism and consequently led to a crisis in basic values in the period of postmodernism.

NSK defines experimental, vanguard art as attempt to individualize the collective, to develop the characteristics, needs and values of individuals within the framework of autonomous social organizations—what they call constructive organizations, or what I might call the experimental expressive machines of the multitudes. From the viewpoint of exploding Yugoslavia in 1991, at a time when it was politically necessary to reflect on the form that such social organizations could take, NSK attempted to exorcize the totalitarian state, and to replay the traumatic history of vanguards, so as to recover their potential autonomy. This led to the theatrical and symbological mimesis of Stalinism and above all Nazism, in the performances for which the group is primarily famous. It would be unfortunate, however, to stop at this pseudo-ritual stage of "casting out the demons," and yet worse, to fetishize its specific historical contents. NSK's identification with vanguards at the moment of their absorption by the totalitarian state only takes on its full meaning when coupled with the forward-looking proposal of a society-building process of individuation, emerging precisely from a collective context. Questioning the very consistency of the state—its spatial and temporal modes of being—was, for NSK, a strategy of freedom.

At present, I believe that an ambition for sophisticated and concentrated art is to exorcize the institutional forms of transnational state capitalism, which has appropriated and distorted the experimentalism of the period around 1968. This theatrical, stylistic and psychic exorcism (the word is not too strong) supposes a corresponding material reality: the construction of expressive machines that can project, exchange and elaborate the imaginaries of a society where collective infrastructure actually favors individuation, rather than reducing it to the servile caricatures of postmodern individualism (and indeed, "collectivity") demanded for integration to the current managerial structures. In fact, this kind of work has already appeared, if one considers the Bureau of Inverse Technology in the United States, Yo Mango in Spain (and the "Mapas" group[24]), 0100101110101101.org in Italy, Bureau d'Études in France, and a host of others, of which ®™ark and the Yes Men are no doubt the most exemplary—particularly because they show no dependence on the control structures of the really existing aesthetic institutions. The symbolic violence exercised by these groups dissolves, at best, into a contagious humor and an imaginary of active, critical emancipation, conveyed by sophisticated strategies and techniques of distribution which prefigure the formation of a "non-state public sphere," as called for by Paolo Virno.[25] An experimental public sphere whose multiple and situated participants may be able to imagine, and ultimately even institute, alternatives to the dangerous reduction of any concern for our collective destinies in the world—a reduction now being imposed by the spectacular communication machines of contemporary capitalism.

Notes

1. Cornelius Castoriadis, "Fait et à Faire," in *Fait et à Faire: Les carrefours du labyrinthe V* (Paris: Seuil, 1997), p. 76.
2. Cf. *Fredric Jameson, Postmodernism, or, the Cultural Logic of Late Capitalism* (Durham: Duke UP,1991), esp. this passage: "The end of the bourgeois ego, or monad, no doubt brings with it the end of the psychopathologies of that ego—what I have been calling the waning of affect. But it means the end of much more.... the liberation, in contemporary society, from the older anomie of the centered subject may also mean not merely a liberation from anxiety but a liberation from every other kind of feeling as well, since there is no longer a self present to do the feeling." But Jameson's limit has been to never ask about the possible invention of other kinds of feeling, or of a process of individuation detached from the "bourgeois ego."
3. C. Castoriadis, "Pouvoir, politique, autonomie," in *Le monde morcelé : Les carrefours du labyrinthe III* (Paris: Seuil, 1990), pp. 160–171; similar formulations can be found in, for example, "Phusis and Autonomy," in *World in Fragments: Writings on Politics, Society, Psychoanalysis, and the Imagination*, tr. D. A. Curtis (Stanford: Stanford University Press, 1997), pp. 331-41.
4. Cf. C. Castoriadis, *L'institution imaginare de la société* (Paris: Seuil, 1975), esp. pp. 138–157. English translation: *The Imaginary Institution of Society*, tr. Kathleen Blarney (Cambridge, Mass.: MIT, 1998), pp. 101–114.
5. Castoriadis describes how social invention arises from psychic origins: "It is only insofar as the radical imagination of the psyche succeeds in transpiring through the successive strata of the social armor that is the individual, which covers it up and penetrates it all the way to an unfathomable limit-point, that the singular human being exerts an action in return upon society." "Pouvoir, politique, autonomie," *op. cit.*, p. 140.
6. Bureau d'Ètudes, "Autonomous Knowledge and Power in a Society without Affects," available at www.u-tangente.org.
7. See for yourself at www.indiana.edu/~unionet/people2.htm.

8. Philippe Urfalino, *L'invention de la politique culturelle française* (Paris: La documentation française, 1996).
9. Some primary sources on immaterial labor: A. Corsani, M. Lazzarato, A. Negri, *Le Bassin du travail immateriel (BTI) dans le métropole parisien* (Paris: L'Harmattan, 1996); M. Lazzarato, *Lavoro Immateriale: Forme di vita e produzione della soggetività* (Verona: Ombre Corte Edizioni, 1997); C. Marazzi, *Il posto dei calzini* (Torino: Bollati-Boringhieri, 1999); and in English, the articles by M. Lazzarato, "Immaterial Labor," in *Radical Thought in Italy: A Potential Politics* (Minneapolis: University of Minnesota Press, 1966), and M. Hardt, "Affective Labor," *boundary* 26:2 (January, 1999). Also see the discussion of immaterial labor in A. Negri and M. Hardt, *Empire* (Cambridge: Harvard University Press, 2000).
10. British Government, Department for Culture, Media and Sport, available at: www.culture.gov.uk/global/publications/archive_1998/Creative_Industries_Mapping_Document_1998.htm.
11. Cf. Maurizio Lazzarato, "Créer des mondes," *Multitudes* 15 (Winter 2003); available at: http://multitudes.samizdat.net/article.php3?id_article=1285.
12. For event sponsors see www.tate.org.uk/supportus/corporate/mem_current.htm
13. Cf. Chin-tao Wu, *Privatising Culture: Corporate Art Intervention since the 1980s* (London: Verso, 2002).
14. For the definition of the "Schumpeterian Workfare Postnational Regime"—seeking to optimize the cognitive performance of the most capable citizens on the transnational knowledge markets—see Bob Jessop, *The Future of the Capitalist State* (Cambridge: Polity Press, 2002).
15. For the "financial core" see Bureau d'Études, "The World Government: Post-national states, influence networks, biocracy," brochure, 2004. Available at www.u-tangente.org.
16. See, for example, http://history.etoy.com/stories/entries/42.
17. Luc Boltanski, Eve Chiapello, *Le nouvel esprit du capitalisme* (Paris: Gallimard, 1999), in English as *The New Spirit of Capitalism* (London: Verso, 2005).; Brian Holmes, "The Flexible Personality: For a New Cultural Critique," in *Hieroglyphs of the Future* (Zagreb: Whw/Arkzin, 2002), at: www.u-tangente.org.

18. For the logic of these events, see the Italian site www. chainworkers.org.
19. For further information, see *Multitudes* 17 (Summer 12004), special issue on "Intermittence dans tous ses états,", as well as the article on "Stopub" in *Multitudes* 16 (Spring 2004), both at: http://multitudes.samizdat.net.
20. J.A. Maravall, *Culture of the Baroque* (Minneapolis: University of Minnesota Press, 1993); also see "From the Renaissance to the Baroque: The Diphasic Schema of a Social Crisis," in *Literature Among the Discourses: The Spanish Golden Age* (Minneapolis: The University of Minnesota Press, 1986), eds. W. Godzich and N. Spadaccini.
21. For "symbolic analysts," see Robert Reich, *The Work of Nations: Preparing Ourselves for 21st Century Capitalism* (New York: Vintage, 1992); for the "creative class," Richard Florida, *The Rise of the Creative Class* (New York: Basic Books, 2002). The most precise developments of Deleuze's notion of "control societies" are by M. Lazzarato, *op. cit.*, and Philippe Zarifian, *A quoi sert le travail?* (Paris: La Dispute, 2003), esp. pp. 13–28, and "Contrôle des engagements et productivité sociale," in *Multitudes* 17.
22. C. Castoriadis, *L'institution imaginaire de la société, op. cit.*, p. 141.
23. Texts available at: http://www.nskstate.com/athens/state/state.asp.
24. For one of the most complex and effective projects in recent activism, see www.sindominio.net/mapas.
25. "The general intellect asserts itself as an autonomous public sphere only if the juncture that ties it to the production of goods and wage labor is severed." Paolo Virno, *A Grammar of the Multitude* (New York: Semiotext(e), 2004), p. 68.

EuroMayday 2006

10

A RISING TIDE OF CONTRADICTION

MUSEUMS IN THE AGE OF THE EXPANDING WORKFARE STATES

Imagine a six-story multiplex with reception and ticketing facilities, cinemas, conference and performance halls, media and information centers, libraries, book and gift shop, cafeteria, restaurant/bar and, of course, exhibition galleries: it's the Pompidou Center in Paris. Distribute these functions inside a huge enclosed courtyard, with multiple buildings and all the attractions of an architectural promenade: it's the Museums Quartier in Vienna. Scatter them further within a renovated city whose traditional festivals and contemporary intellectual life can be reprogrammed as events in a tourist calendar: it's the entire municipality of Barcelona. The welfare states may be shrinking, but certainly not the museum. The latter is rather fragmenting, penetrating ever more deeply and organically into the complex mesh of semiotic production. Its spinoff products—design, fashion, multimedia spectacle, but also relational technologies and outside-the-box consulting—are among the driving forces of the contemporary economy. We are far from the modernist notion of the museum as a collection of great works, to be displayed as a public service. Instead, we are talking about proactive laboratories of social transformation. We are talking about museums that work, museums that form part of the dominant economy, and that change at an increasing rate of acceleration imposed by both the market and the state. Is it impossible to use this vast development of cultural activity for anything other than the promotion of tourism, consumption, the batch-processing of human attention and emotion? The answer depends on the availability of two elusive commodities: confrontational practice and constructive critique.

The critique can begin from an understanding of the now almost completed "crisis of the welfare state." Its origin is wrongly attributed to the neoliberal turn in governance that began in the mid-1970s, with Chicago school economics and Thatcher's conservative revolution. But that was only the second phase. The cultural critique of the 1960s was anti-bureaucratic to the core. It sought to dissolve the industrial hierarchies that shaped one's most intimate being. The anthropologist Pierre Clastres summed up this aspiration in a phrase: "Society against the State." And here the neoliberals found their opportunity. They combined a change in economic organization (modular management of semi- or pseudo-autonomous "profit centers," against any vertical integration) with an ambitious new social policy (mobilization of the workforce, not through the promise of social guarantees, but through the personal implication of passion, ethics, subjectivity). Imagination takes command, above and beyond the fading importance of mechanization, while welfare (the guarantee of a certain "free time" away from the machines) is replaced by workfare (a recipe for total mobilization of the population). Art—or more broadly, "creativity"—has become the linchpin of the workfare system, in the financialized era of image and sign production. It is both the icon and the mode of inclusion to the present society, which attempts to drive everyone to constantly escalating levels of activity. Or to drive them into the margins, if they can't be made to fit. In this way, the cultural multiplex bears witness to a Hegelian ruse of history. Amidst the profusion of commercialized aesthetics, the individual revolt of generations past has been integrated, as a vector and mask of repressive exclusion. But we shall not escape this fate by any return to state-run bureaucracies, to religiously silent modernist museums. What must be invented instead is a radically different form of governmentality—whereby, as Foucault said, free subjects seek to "conduct the conduct of others."

Of what does confrontational practice consist today? It consists of the autonomous, deliberately inefficient and de-normalized production of aesthetic devices, to disrupt and derail the attention-channeling techniques brought to bear by the partnerships of the workfare state and corporate capital. The Mayday parades of flexible workers, invented in Milan and now in Barcelona, are paradigmatic examples. They begin from the multiple forms of exclusion—the undocumented, the unemployed, squatters' movements, people without various forms of insurance, people without any possibility of collective bargaining—and attempt to build a political consciousness of the labor-and-living situation, while striking out at the most characteristic forms of oppression and exploitation. Their means are, of course, aesthetic: for this is how the members of our societies "conduct the conduct of others," at least in the relatively protected Imperial centers. But this is an aesthetics of carnival, of chaos. The Mayday parades use cooperative, solidarity-based forms of organization to mobilize the energies of equals, joined in chaotic confrontation against the carefully calculated images of the brands and the touristic environments, which manage and channel behavior to foreclose any political speech. The image of pink-feathered dancers expressively disrupting the commerce of a Zara store in Milan sums up this new combat perfectly. But so does a Spanish video, "Desmantelando Indra," showing the entry of a group of protestors, dressed as weapons inspectors, to the offices of an arms manufactory, followed by the deliberate disassembly of all the communications and computer equipment, left quarantined in sealed cardboard boxes which read "Danger: Weapons of Mass Destruction" (www.sindominio.net/mapas/es/accions_es.htm).

Corporate communications as deadly weapons in a global civil war: this is exactly what is hidden by the fashion industry's "Weapons of Mass Deception." At stake is the deconstruction of the war economy, and the creation of a collective basis for the voluntary forms of free cooperation (transformed housing, insurance, transportation, and labor regimes, new forms of socialized access to communications equipment, copyleft rights to the commons, the invention of collective forms of property, the expansion of subsidiarity and direct democratic procedures). And Mayday-style emergency activism is only the most obvious figure of the new spaces opening up for confrontational experimentation. All around us—but more modestly, slowly, discreetly—similar energies are in action, at softer, subtler, more intimate levels, where the psychic meets the artistic and the political.

What could a museum contribute to this kind of aesthetic activism? First, its genealogy, which runs in an unbroken line from the earliest dada experiments (developed amidst the butchery of the First World War) all way through the sequences of installationist practice, happenings, conceptual art, situationist intervention (themselves developed amidst the Vietnam War and the uproar of the '68 movements). A genealogy of art that seeks to go beyond itself, art for the outside. But second, the museum can also give the activist forms their opening to debate, not as dead corpses of the past for academic dissection, but as inspirations and reference-points for the development of new practices in the immediate future. The post-workfare institution, rather than grafting a repository of useless modern expertise onto an up-to-date stimulator for consuming motivations, becomes a sensuous library of alternatives to the total capitalist mobilization of society. It's an archive that doesn't require silence from its users. In a third contribution, it projects certain resources beyond its walls, to engage in experimentation and exchange amidst the texture of competing aesthetics that is the contemporary city. It gathers traces of this and other autonomous activity. It works to connect spaces, both physical and electronic, in which such traces can become the object of open, prospective discussion. So doing it helps fulfill the ambitions of most contemporary art, all the claims to be a miniaturized model of social interactions, an undetermined field for their reinvention. But instead of sterilizing that promise within exclusive, highly class-determined boundaries, and instead of reducing its production to objects-for-contemplation, it recognizes the fundamental conflicts within society, and engages risky procedures which can help release those conflicts from confinement to violent dead ends, raising them instead to the political level where equals confront equals. The level where governmentality is a collective issue. Here is the public-service role of the new "museums." It is fulfilled, exemplarily, by a micro-institution such as Public Netbase, notably in the container-operations recently mounted on Vienna's Karlsplatz, and in all their electronic echoes. But it also exists as a virtuality, in the desire of thousands of institutional actors who are disappointed and revolted by the operations of the cultural multiplexes, and the failing model of public service as it was conceived by the welfare state.

How can the virtual become actual? What's lacking at this point is less the artistic practice, than a strong criticism that can inscribe criteria of value and decision within both the public and the professional debates. After five years of the most intense social and artistic activism, we have yet to develop a constructive critique. The criticism of the magazines and curators remains pathetically servile ("affirmative," in Marcuse's phrase), while minority developments remain caught either in the trap of disillusionment and cynical observation of the disaster, or in the marginally preferable impasse of pure radicalism and refusal of anything that smacks of cooptation. It is true that critique, like confrontational practice, must take on the attributes of a commodity whenever it is accepted within the confines of the institutional market. And this is a problem, for real. But cooptation is also an open front of social struggle. The notion that this struggle could be won through the appeal to pure forms of democratic discussion and communicational reason (Habermas) has proven as illusory as perverse hopes in the ability of market-governed production to translate popular aspirations (Cultural Studies). There is no "solution" for a leftist cultural position within a market society, but instead, an ongoing tension between the actors inside and outside the institutions, at the oft-crossed limits of the breaking-point. Today it seems that a continually problematic movement between what Diego Stzulwark and Miguel Benasayag once called "situations of resistance" and "situations of management"—seized in their irresolvable contradiction—offers the only chance of doing something with a plethora of aesthetic institutions captured by the rising tide of the contemporary workfare state.

Jakob Boeskov, The ID Sniper, 2004

11
SIGNALS, STATISTICS & SOCIAL EXPERIMENTS

THE GOVERNANCE CONFLICTS OF ELECTRONIC MEDIA ART

The term "governmentality," coined some twenty-five years ago by Michel Foucault, describes what is essentially a feedback process: the endlessly renegotiated balances of a "microphysics of power" in which each individual contributes a vital force to the production of the social frameworks that condition his or her behavior. Under this view, power does not just come down on a population from above, that is, from the state and those whose interests it serves. Rather, it also arises from the activity of those whose invention and conviction are required to shape the prevailing usages and norms. Thus the substantial reality of citizenship, for a governmentality theorist like Nikolas Rose, does not only consist of participation in a formal "public sphere," where enfranchised individuals debate over the dispositions and meanings of universal law. Instead, "games of citizenship" are played out in the most diverse arenas:

> The citizen as consumer is to become an active agent in the regulation of professional expertise. The citizen as prudent is to become an active agent in the provision of security. The citizen as employee is to become an active agent in the regeneration of industry and as consumer is to be an agent for innovation, quality and competitiveness.... This kind of "government through freedom" multiplies the points at which the citizen has to play his or her part in the games that govern him. And, in doing so, it also multiplies the points at which citizens are able to refuse, contest, challenge those demands that are placed upon them.[1]

The strength of Rose's work is to have retraced in detail some of the procedures that have been developed since WWI for conceiving a population's self-conduct in psychological terms, observing and measuring its variability, inscribing it as statistics, and then calculating the effects of the government programs, advertising messages and market offers that are designed to channel it in specific directions. On one hand, these are procedures for producing the truth, that is to say, establishing so-called scientific criteria for normalizing people's behavior. But the claim being made in the analysis of governmentality is that a large degree of hitherto unsuspected freedom lies in the continually changing subjective production of that which can only be guided, directed, cajoled and seduced from the outside, i.e. self-conduct. Here is the source of the Deleuzean dictum that "resistance is primary," along with the corresponding theory of social control by "apparatuses of capture"—two ideas that have inspired much recent social theory.

However, instead of just celebrating the breakthrough that such ideas effectively represent, one could ask about the specific kinds of games that we have begun to play today, in the age of the so-called new media. For our embrace, as a population, of miniaturized, networked electronic devices, has made us into avid producers of signals, emanating from all aspects of our psychic, sexual, professional, political and affective lives. These signals of belief and desire are eminently susceptible to interception, storage in databases, and transformation into statistics, which can be used as guidelines for the informed manipulation of our environment, and thus of our behavior. It then becomes important to know what kinds of social experiments we might be part of.

And I will go further: it becomes important to produce counter-experiments, to up the stakes of the game, to deploy the primacy of resistance in the key arenas of our epoch. This could be a worthwhile use for the relative autonomy of the new media centers, festivals, exhibitions and educational programs. That is, it could be, if participants can find the inventions, the critical discourses and the political will to assert their autonomy in the face of their funders—i.e. the state and the electronics industries.

Consider the case of Jakob Boeskov and his pseudo-company "Empire North," which signed up in 2002 as the sole Danish exhibitor at "China Police 2002"—the first international weapons fair in the People's Republic. Empire North's security product took the form of a prototype, advertised on a poster under the name *ID Sniper*. The poster, displayed at the empty stall that a trembling and uncertain Boeskov occupied at China Police 2002, contained this explanation:

> The idea is to implant a GPS microchip in the body of a human being, using a high-powered sniper rifle as the long distance injector.... At the same time, a digital camcorder with a zoom lens fitted within the scope will take a high-resolution picture of the target. This picture will be stored on a memory card for later image-analysis. GPS microchip technology is already being used for tracking millions of pets in various countries, and the logical solution is to use it on humans as well, when the situation demands it....
>
> As the urban battlefield grows more complex and intense, new ways of managing and controlling crowds are needed. The attention of the media changes the rules of the game. Sometimes it is difficult to engage the enemy in the streets without causing damage to the all-important image of the state. Instead, Empire North suggests marking and identifying a suspicious subject from a safe distance, enabling the national law enforcement agency to keep track on the target through a satellite in the weeks to come.[2]

Jakob Boeskov is an artist, a young but obviously politicized one, satirizing the excesses of his state and corporate nemeses through a radical form of what Slavoj Zizek calls "over-identification." He took an undeniable risk to realize his project, and by his own account became almost unbearably afraid when, for instance, a French diplomat pointed out the impossibility of the weapon, given the damage it would inevitably cause to the internal organs of protesting citizens. Nonetheless, the heart of his proposal—the miniature radio frequency ID tag to be injected in the bodies of the demonstrators—is quite real. It is produced by a company called "Applied Digital Solutions." It is sold under the trade name "VeriChip."[3] It is offered in several different packages: "VeriTrack" for continuous surveillance of mobile materiel and personnel; and "VeriGuard," an implanted, infra-cutaneous access badge which "cannot be forgotten, lost or stolen." Verification guaranteed. This bit of silicon and wire is a technology for producing effective truth. And as of October 13, 2004, it has been cleared by the American Food and Drug Administration for health-care use in the United States.

The chips are supposed to provide "easy access to individual medical records." But that apparently benign application could smooth the way for others, as is so often the case with surveillance technologies: "Applied Digital Solutions of Delray Beach, Fla., said that its devices, which it calls VeriChips, could save lives and limit injuries from errors in medical treatment. It hopes such medical uses will accelerate acceptance of under-the-skin ID chips as security and access-control devices." Of course, Old Europeans will rest assured that only the U.S. could condone such a barbaric idea, developed for control and security. On the Continent it is pure pleasure that provides the necessary legitimacy: "In March, the Baja Beach Club in Barcelona, Spain, began offering VeriChips to regular patrons who want to dispense with traditional identification and credit cards. About 50 'VIPs' have received the chip so far, according to a company spokesman, which allows them to link their identities to a payment system."[4] One man's whisky is as good as another man's medicine it seems—and both are sufficient excuses to get surveillance chips under our collective skin.

The disturbing thing is how easily such invasive technologies are accepted and made into norms. Under these conditions, the work of an artist like Boeskov becomes a rare chance to actually play the governance game, by opening up a public space for refusing, contesting and challenging these new tracking and recording regimes. To make such challenges effective on a broader scale, however, at least three requirements would have to be fulfilled. First, high-risk projects like *The ID Sniper* would have to be accepted as valid and ongoing experiments within the new-media institutions. Second, controversies around them would have to be produced, with a maximum number of participants, and not only in the realms of discourse. And third, the artists involved would have to be defended, when their investigations of corporate and state experiments succeed in generating the all-too predictable repression.

COUNTER-EXPERIMENTS

How can artists—or anyone else for that matter—possibly respond to the strategies of normalization? The obvious critique of governmentality theory is that ordinary citizens have no imaginable chance to accumulate the vast amounts of data that state and corporate actors hold on them. Their desires and usages can provide the vital thrust of an initial transformation; but subsequent expressions will unfold within the established frameworks, to the point where "expression" itself comes to feel programmed, solicited and channeled by the manipulated environment. And of course, the procedures for stacking the deck of governmentality are nothing new. Nikolas Rose goes back to the 1920s to show how the normalizing gaze of the psychological researcher comes to fall on earliest infancy, scrutinizing the gestures of the gurgling baby and recording them on film in order to produce abstracted and codified models of behavior (plates 1-3, pp. 146-49). The cool efficiency of this gaze is one of the sources of intense alienation experienced by industrialized populations in the 1950s and 1960s, always unsure of which technocratic mirror may have been installed at the heart of their subjectivity. A 1974 installation by the artist Dan Graham, under the title *Present Continuous Past(s)*, provides a public experience of this disturbing tension between fluid self-presence and the return of the technocratic gaze. We see our image in an ordinary mirror, where it is as mobile as life itself; but at the same time, and in the same mirror, we see a video device continually projecting a surveillance-camera recording from eight seconds before, haunting our present experience and informing it with its own capture. The question of how one will play out this game between the spontaneity of the present and the recorded traces of the past is at the center of this paradigmatic artwork, which is nothing other than a meta-model of innumerable social experiments.

It would be interesting to reconsider the production of the postwar installationists, to see to what extent the feedback loops of governmentality became an issue in their devices. Another artist one would soon encounter is Bruce Nauman, whose long-term obsession with behaviorism becomes explicit in a late installation like *Rats and Bats (On Learned Helplessness in Rats)*, from 1988. The piece takes the form of a yellow plastic labyrinth, using video monitors (in the place of the traditional bait that lures laboratory rats through the maze) and a soundtrack of painfully loud rock'n'roll drumming (in the place of the traditional electroshock). The commercial media are staged as the determining stimuli of a social experiment. But the pathos of Nauman's art betrays all the melancholy of the objective and objectifying model; and it culminates in his anguished emphasis on "withdrawal," which is precisely the syndrome that postwar industrial psychologists sought to cure in the alienated worker.[5] Perhaps one would then have to extend the inquiry to the full range of artistic resistance to normalization, from the resurgence in the 1950s of concrete poetry—with its corporeal and respiratory foundation for direct human expression—through cut-up and montage procedures conceived against televisual continuity, to the political psychodrama of Oyvind Fahlström's game-pieces and the orchestrated deviance of 1960s happenings, then on to the experimental media work of artists like Nam June Paik. These are just a few of the ways that artists engage in an active resistance to formatted behavior, and in a channeling of alternatives—literally, in Paik's case, with the famous satellite-relay video piece of 1973 entitled *Global Groove*.

The examples I'm quoting here are canonical, they are found in textbooks and in prestigious white cubes. But they and many others could be used as a genealogy, leading through a history of twentieth-century art in its subtly or explicitly conflictual relation to what the sociologist Alain Touraine once called "the programmed society." What could be recovered from such a genealogy is the symbolic and practical antagonism that pits one kind of social experiment against another. This is the kind of game that can unfold within the computerized media, where the contemporary forms of data-gathering are practiced, and where the new control regimes are being imposed, through the use of truth-producing devices like the VeriChip. But an interesting conflict rarely just happens—particularly since contemporary art itself has now been normed, organized, channeled into the safe-havens of museums. The debate must be created, extended, deepened and resolved in public, where the issues themselves exist.

PRODUCING THE CONTROVERSY

If interventionist projects have a much greater intensity today than the purely symbolic constructions of older artistic models, it's for a simple reason: the attraction of the reality show. What matters in *ID Sniper* is the fact that Boeskov was there, and beyond that, the fact that you might go there someday soon. What matters is that the effects of the international arms economy are shockingly real. So there's no use to cry out against populism and withdraw into hermetic abstraction. Much better is the production of an intelligent event, bringing reality to a more complex and challenging level of display. Activists have always known how to do this. A great example is the projection onto the building of the World Intellectual Property Foundation in Geneva, Switzerland, of the video by the San Francisco group Negativeland, *Gimme the Mermaid*, which deliberately infringes on the copyright of Disney.[6] The screening on the WIPO building in the context of the World Summit on the Information Society in December 2003 could hardly been more significant, where the intellectual property game is concerned. But the event itself was seen by a relatively small number of people and probably understood by even fewer; it has to be distributed. And this could be the real role of the institution in the process of contemporary governance.

Take a rare example: the Public Netbase in Vienna.[7] Two recent projects have been exemplary: *Nikeground*, by 0100101110101101.org, and *System 77 Civil Counter-Reconnaissance* initiative, by Marko Peljhan. Both events were held on the Karlsplatz, under conditions of semi-legality that contributed to the meaning of the display. The first went up against a powerful transnational corporation, to undercut the norm of logo-typing that installs corporate worlds as the very earth beneath our feet. It proposed renaming the historic city square, installing a gigantic swoosh sculpture to redefine the notion of public art, and of course, providing a new style of shoe to put you into intimate contact with the transfigured ground of your existence. The second project took on the issues of sophisticated surveillance techniques as the exclusive prerogative of the state. It proposed a civilian appropriation of unmanned aerial vehicles (UAVs) to restore the balance between the citizens and the police. In both cases it was necessary to engage with local bureaucrats and politicians, so as to push the artistic fiction into the media and prolong the uncertainty surrounding its kernel of truth. Only by sparring with private interests and public authorities, while at the same time distributing information and disinformation through every attainable channel, could Public Netbase give either of these two projects the presence they need—if they are even to begin to interfere with the ordinary games of governance. But is the media-art community capable of supporting such radical initiatives?

DEFENDING THE TRICKSTERS

The answer, on the institutional level at least, is that things don't look particularly good. Public Netbase has seen the constant trimming of its operational budget by center-left administrations, despite the promises made during its high-profile resistance to the Haider governments. Now it looks like this impressive new-media laboratory is going to definitively close its doors, having recently laid off its entire staff and ceased its operations. Meanwhile in the USA, Steve Kurtz of Critical Art Ensemble is on trial before a federal grand jury for a technicality concerning the way that he obtained a perfectly harmless sample of *E. coli* bacteria. What kind of social truth is going to be produced by that grand jury? Support of all kinds is urgently needed, because the basic strategy of such political trials is to wear out the resources of citizens over the long term, both in terms of cash and of critical attention.[8] At a certain point, money and expert assistance become the feedback loops that really matter.

These sorry situations are indicative of the immeasurably broader state of world affairs, which is not going to turn around too quickly. It's all very well to feel optimistic about governmentality theory, and to talk about power rising from below. But the question of what exactly happens on the way up can no longer be overlooked. Much more concerted efforts will have to be made, at a higher level of critique and political demand, if we want to keep a few experimental arenas open in the worlds of art, media and activism, to go on exploring the possibility of governing ourselves otherwise.

Notes

1. Nikolas Rose, *Governing the Soul* (London: Free Association Books, 2nd edition, 1999), p. xxiii.
2. http://events.thing.net/Boeskov_text.html; see Boeskov's site at http://backfire.dk/EMPIRENORTH/newsite.
3. www.4verichip.com
4. Barnaby J. Feder and Tom Zeller Jr., "Identity Badge Worn Under Skin Approved for Use in Health Care," *New York Times*, October 14, 2004.
5. Cf. *Governing the Soul,* chapter 8, pp. 90–94.
6. The video is available at www.illegal-art.org/video/popups/gimme.html. An account of the projection, with photo links, is here: www.geneva03.org/polimedia/display.php?id=278&lang=en.
7. www.t0.or.at/t0; the websites of the specific projects discussed are: www.nikeground.com and www.s-77ccr.org.
8. www.caedefensefund.org

Marko Peljhan, S-77CCR, 2004

12

S-77CCR

EYES IN THE SKIES, DEMOCRACY IN THE STREETS

C urious? So Are We...

Eyebrows will rise at the sight of an ultramodern communications tower pointing up from historic Karlsplatz like an extended middle finger. But what better way to say, the real issues are above your heads? Already with the intensification of civil dissent throughout the Western democracies in the 1990s, the Cold War surveillance system began a process of involution, miniaturizing and proliferating into our daily lives. The security panic after the events of S&M-11 has done the rest. Advanced electronic and biometric equipment, transported on unmanned aerial vehicles (UAVs), can now be used against peaceful demonstrators in the homeland cities. Every cloud may not have a silver lining—but it is likely to conceal an agent of the police. Protests such as those that were held in Vienna against the Haider government on February 4, 2000, may already be obsolete.

Faced with the electromagnetic specter of the unknown, human-rights groups have decided to seize extraordinary market opportunities, and equip themselves with the latest in airborne imaging devices, radio communications vectors and geographic information systems (GIS), to locate and track the adversaries (our public-service administrations) even as they are locating and tracking *you*. The result is *System-77 Civilian Counter Reconnaissance: Eyes in the skies, for democracy in the streets*.

SURVEILLANCE IS FREEDOM

Just look at the precision of the computerized city plans, the high-resolution detail of the surging crowds, the instantaneous breadth of perspective and control afforded by the drone's eye view. And imagine the exhilarating sense of mission on the morning of the big demo, when *you* get to be the mobile operator of a 1.8 meter-long AeroVironment Pointer—"a production-ready electric UAV designed for reconnaissance, surveillance and remote monitoring." Purchased straight off the Internet just like the Interior Ministry procurement services do, this elegant, ultra-light, glider-like drone can be hand-launched like an ancient Greek hurling a javelin into the azurean blue. Of course the classical philosophers had never heard of airborne transmitter-equipped video cameras the size of a penny, let alone thermal imaging systems for infrared night-vision. But the fundamental issues remain the same: democracy, citizenship and freedom. With one or several UAVs controlled by real-time synthetic vision, feeding video captures and GIS map-readouts to a portable, radio-linked computer, civil society at last obtains the information advantage enjoyed by the secret services, the army or the police. Top-down surveillance for grassroots initiatives! Wireless Internet connections allow for distributed access to locational data on officer concentrations, suspicious van movements or impending water-cannon deployment; and cell-phone trees plus SMS texting do the rest, transforming an easily immobilized and frustrated crowd into a fast-moving, polymorphous swarm of intelligent agents with at least a running chance to exercise their right to free speech.

Sometimes it's hard to believe we ever did without these devices. But of course, those were the days before government became a mirror of enterprise, and before private security companies began training public officials in how to keep the peace. Now in advanced countries like the USA, it's illegal to obstruct traffic on the sidewalk! Under such conditions, pragmatic idealists use every tool that progress makes available. And technology moves fast today. Path-breaking projects like MIT's "Government Information Awareness" already seem almost passé. Why know the dirt on your elected fascist representatives, if you can't avoid a squad of precision-guided officers on your way to a public demonstration? And who will watch the watchdogs, as the Roman writer Juvenal used to say?

STIMUFACTION GUARANTEED

Underinformed citizens might be disturbed by seeming parallels between legitimate counter-reconnaissance work and the aerial tactics of groups like Al-Qaeda ("The Base"). Of course we could note that civilian reconnaissance planes have an impressive safety record, and are rarely known to explode. Yet recent third-level democracy studies give some credence to citizens' spontaneous intuition, though at a higher of order of abstraction, as they say. Because the little-known fact is that military surveillance technologies have not only been spun off into the private security industry, but also into the commercial arena. Behind the familiar Universal Product Code on the goods you buy, for instance, there is probably a radio frequency identification tag (RFID), which serves among other things to record your purchasing habits and your movements through the store. Combined with credit- and loyalty-card statistics garnered at the checkout desk, plus a host of personal details purchased on the open info-markets (loans and insurance stats, medical records, employment history, travel and viewing preferences), this kind of in-store surveillance helps to flesh out your databody, to track your most intimate desires, so that a full-fledged consumer world can be tailored to fit. And why not conceal those RFID tags inside the products, so further user-profiles can be gleaned in every situation?

Accelerated progress in the micromanagement of individual "stimufaction" (stimulation/satisfaction as a near-perfect coincidence) means that reality is no longer an obstacle to the advertising teams, and an entire civilizational spectacle based on exploited immigrant labor and imported Middle-Eastern oil can be promoted as the only imaginable future. With or without further American improvements in electronic voting machines, electoral outcomes on the Old Continent are guaranteed: nothing will be done to change the imperialist economy, even when extremely unequal exchange gives rise to proliferating terrorism. The imposition of biometric technologies (retinal scan, digital fingerprint, vocal reconnaissance, human odor signatures), first required at international borders, then at cash machines, public buildings, workplace turnstiles, and finally at your own apartment door, swerves to cement the feeling of no escape—so why not enjoy the simulacrum? Under such conditions, the turn to hi-tech interactive civil disobedience becomes the only possible continuation of democracy. Albeit by radically different means.

SWARMING THE HEAVENS

The security system faces a few small problems nonetheless. For one, conventional censorship and media manipulation from above are clearly obsolete—as proved by the recent Spanish bombing, when voters refused, not only their country's participation in the Iraq war, but above all their leader's attempt to grossly misrepresent reality, by directly muzzling the watchdogs of a once-free press. But Western intelligence hardly awaited the networked demonstrations on the eve of the Spanish elections to conclude that hypermobile swarming was the wave of the future. Thus the struggle for UAV dominance already intensifies, before it has even really begun. Third-level democracy consultants quiver before the prospect of massive launches, by both civilians and police, of Miniature Aerial Vehicles (MAVs), such as the infamous Black Widow. Weighing only 50 grams, but of course camera-equipped and fully interactive, the Widow weaves an intelligent net of evasive surveillance when launched in a swarm, whether by officers or demonstrators. In combination with clouds of RFID "motes," reduced to microscopic size and dispersed into the clothing or hair of the rival teams, widow-like MAVs knit an electronic fabric of surveillant struggle beyond the wildest dreams of the late 1990s, even if that period was obsessed with the subject.

The obvious question—*where will it all end?*—becomes increasingly difficult to ask, in a market-driven environment where each new conflict bears an aura of obsolescence before even properly beginning. But if we accept the third-level analysts' central tenet—namely, that the productive machinery of the former Cold War has involuted to a highly profitable Virtual Civil Repression (VCR), pressed forward under the urgently real pretext of terror—then there may be some wisdom to be salvaged from the dustbin of East-West history.

It is well known that both sides in the Cold War conflict achieved matching levels of Mutually Assured Destruction, making any further extension of their atomic arsenals reciprocally insane (MAD). Less well known is the degree to which double-spies, moles, worms and other intelligence paradoxes gradually rendered the comprehensibility of everyday affairs almost nil, resulting in the collapse of the Cold War paradigm. Is it too much to suppose that the opposing logics of networked reconnaissance and counter reconnaissance—or "swarm versus swarm," to update an older figure—should soon or perhaps already have rendered contemporary urban conflicts entirely senseless? How much simulated posturing is required, before the contemporary surveillance game reaches the critical threshold of Mutually Assured Deception? Is there any preemptive chance to actually *perceive the world situation*, before embarking on a new and even more intensive round of planetary shadow-boxing which can only profit the military-entertainment complex—that is to say, a few well-placed politician-generals, and a considerably larger number of rapacious corporations?

Brian Holmes, Ph.D.
Third-Level Demo-Consultant
Public Netbase t0 / World-Information.org
Official project website: s-77ccr.org

13

THREE PROPOSALS FOR A REAL DEMOCRACY

INFORMATION-SHARING TO A DIFFERENT TUNE

Since their invention a few years ago, p2p file-sharing networks for the free exchange of music have been the gadfly of consumer capitalism. Puncturing the profits of the recording industry, they have brought unlimited pop to teenagers' lives, and an ironic smile to the lips of those Internet purists who always scorned the profit-seeking illusions of the "new economy." For the politically minded—and particularly the older set, who still equate guitars with protest movements—this massive transgression of copyright law could make it seem like a long-awaited breath of cultural revolt was in the air. But there was just one problem: Who would pay the piper? How would the artists (and, some added, the recording companies) survive in a world of free music? Recently, quite a narrow range of solutions have been proposed: either pay-per-song download sites, in a centralizing scheme favored by the music industry; or a "flatrate" tax on Internet users, preserving file-sharing by providing a source of monetary compensation to be distributed among the copyright holders. One of the flatrate proposals, specifically addressed to the EU's Internal Market Directorate, makes this case for peer-to-peer technologies: "The digital revolution holds the potential of a semiotic democracy, the reuse and remix culture being one of its most promising innovative aspects."[1] So let's ask a question: exactly what's being promised here? And above all, how to get it? How to move from a semiotic to a real democracy?

Take another example of the digital revolution: the call for electronic publication of scientific and scholarly journals, by groups like the Public Library of Science or the Budapest Open Access Initiative.[2] Such publication projects have received extensive support from scholars and scientists, as they would eliminate the barriers to the exchange of knowledge represented by skyrocketing costs for peer-reviewed print journals, which have become prohibitively expensive even for many universities in the developed world. Together with guidelines for self-archiving (i.e. electronic publication without peer review), these initiatives promise the (re)creation of what certain theorists have begun to call an "information commons,"[3] resulting in a major transfer of knowledge from the wealthier institutions to their poorer cousins, and ultimately, from the North to the South. Of course, we are still talking about purely semiotic freedoms. But what might arise from the "reuse and remix" of scientific knowledge? Well, technological development, for one thing. And there, the need to go beyond a semiotic democracy is obvious.

Consider the case of highly expensive AIDS drugs. The knowledge and technology required to manufacture these medicines at low cost is already widely available. But the capacity to do so is limited by patent-protection regimes established on a global scale by the World Intellectual Property Organization (WIPO) and the TRIPS agreement (Trade-Related Aspects of Intellectual Property Rights) of the WTO. It's against international law to save poor people's lives with rich people's science. Nonetheless, the combined efforts of AIDS activists, NGOs, health ministries in the underdeveloped countries, and risk-taking manufacturers such as Cipla in India, led to the deliberate transgression of the patent regimes (in 2001, Cipla could offer its tritherapy generics to Medecins sans Frontieres for a cost of $340 a year per patient, compared to $10,400 for the high end of the trademarked medicines).[4] The result of this activism was the WTO's historic Doha Declaration, which granted exceptions to the TRIPS provisions on patent law in the case of "national emergencies," specifically including epidemics of AIDS, malaria and tuberculosis.[5] Yet the intent of the declaration is now being blocked, by collusion between the transnational drug industry and the current US administration.[6] Intellectual property laws make it difficult to realize the promise of free information exchange.

Why are the hidden connections between file-sharing (in everyday life), open publishing (in scientific and scholarly disciplines) and the transfer of vitally needed technologies (in North-South relations) not immediately obvious to large numbers of people? Or in other words: Why is the democratic promise of the Internet (or the digital revolution) so broadly ignored? Let's go back to the departure point: solutions to the "problem" of free music. A member of the Pirate Bay project, Rasmus Fleischer, has a critique of the flatrate proposal, and specifically, of its claim to offer compensation to property-rights holders without exerting any control over users:

> The record industry builds its power and its business model upon the ability to control people's musical preferences, and it's damn important for them not to loose their grip over that. It seems unsure how long they could go on motivating their existence in a situation where they do not themselves control how music is packaged and presented, what kinds of collection albums and boxes are marketed, when the different singles of an album are released in different parts of the world, etc. In fact, one could say that the music industry needs the money that current copyright laws grant them precisely in order to exercise control.[7]

Fleischer puts a finger on exactly what most advocates of free file-sharing fail to mention: what's being massively exchanged over p2p systems are not independently developed works like open-source software, but commercially produced pop tunes which form a part of today's control culture. In contemporary societies, the word "control" can serve to designate the ways that exclusive property rights over potentially common goods are defended from effective critique, through a carefully orchestrated media modulation of attention, memory and belief. We're no longer talking about ideology as a single, totalizing worldview, and Debord's description of the spectacle society was still too general, too imprecise; what we find in reality is a rivalrous mesh of solicitations, distractions, incitements, all reinforcing different aspects of the basic set of social roles that shape our productivity and desire. Maurizio Lazzarato describes the ways that corporations "create worlds" for their workers and consumers, and engage in "aesthetic wars" to maintain their attractive power and belief-inducing consistency:

> It is enough to turn on the television or the radio, go for a walk in a city, buy a weekly or daily newspaper, to know that this world is constructed through a statement-assemblage, through a sign regime, the expression of which is called advertising; and what is expressed (the meaning) is a prompt or a command, which in themselves are a valuation, a judgment, a belief about the world, about oneself and others. What is expressed (the meaning) is not an ideological valuation, but rather an incentive (it gives signs), a prompt to assume a form of living, i.e. a way of dressing, having a body, eating, communicating, residing, moving, having a gender, speaking, etc.[8]

The creation of rhythmically modulated worlds of sensation and desire is easy enough to grasp in the case of pop-music consumption-and innocuous enough, you might think. A more pointed example would be the endless streams of advertising for pharmaceutical products, offering a longer and healthier life, modulating moods and intimating the promise of vitality, even ecstasy. But advertising is just part of the control equation. Consider the complex opinion-shaping operations required to maintain the belief that the sky-high prices of pharmaceutical products are justified, even when the scientific discoveries that underlie them have most often been made at public universities, using public funds (as is notably the case in the United States). The classic argument-repeated in the media whenever necessary-is that it costs a total of $500 to $800 million to develop, test and produce a new drug, expenditures beyond the reach of any public research institution. However, those figures are provided by a lobby, the Pharmaceutical Research and Manufacturers of America, and by a research center which receives 65% of its funding directly from the industry; real costs are probably a small fraction of the claimed amount. When pressed by a South African court to open their books and prove the research costs which justify their need for exclusive patents on AIDS drugs, thirty-nine pharmaceutical companies preferred to withdraw their suit against the manufacture and distribution of generic medicines.[9] Such cases threaten the industry's manipulation of our belief; yet it remains a $400 billion business worldwide, the third most profitable in 2003 (down from first in 2001 and 2002). Marcia Angell makes this remark: "The most startling fact about 2002 is that the combined profits for the ten drug companies in the Fortune 500 ($35.9 billion) were more than the profits for all the other 490 businesses put together ($33.7 billion)."[10] The good life isn't exactly free these days.

So what are the melodies that big pharma would like us to hear? One that entices, another that deceives, and a third that motivates—like the sound of a jackpot tinkling in the till. Among the neoliberal transformations of the public sector is the way that research is conducted. In the United States (which Europharma envies[11]), the results of research conducted with federal money can be patented by the university and licensed exclusively to private start-ups, which then sell their patented technologies to major corporations; inventors receive a portion of the licensing revenues and may also have an interest in the new business.[12] Withholding publication for patent protection has therefore become increasingly frequent.[13] In this way, the culture of privatization subtly controls the availability and applications of research—but also the very motivation and desire of researchers, who are encouraged to seek their own profit rather than to share knowledge as a public good.

A bit of common knowledge applies here: "He who pays the piper, calls the tune." But when the payments have become structural, when they involve a vast, interlocking system of regulations, interests, strategies and seductions, then a change in the controlling rhythms of social experience requires the introduction of something fundamentally different, entirely outside the prevailing systems of payment (or extortion) that characterize cognitive capitalism.[14] The free exchange of music files has that something—not so much in the branded tunes as in the fact of free exchange, outside a market structured overwhelmingly in the favor of exclusive rightsholders and monopolistic corporations. And each file exchanged is a gift that challenges not just one industry (the recording business), but the whole institution of intellectual property. Nonetheless, if we are to make something of this upsurge of the commons in immediate daily experience, it must be linked to a wider program for the transformation of what are now the basic rules of social interchange. This entails inventing and instituting the conditions for the production and distribution of alternative forms of journalism, scientific and scholarly knowledge, but also cultural creations such as music, literature and the visual arts. Such alternative forms, in all their diversity and intricacy, can also become war machines of a new and astonishing kind, in the discursive and aesthetic struggle to create the worlds in which we live. What we need today, on the Left, is to transform the possibilities of semiotic play, stimulated by the "digital revolution," into a far-ranging, multi-leveled, but above all communicable and workable program for a real democracy.

To do this requires surmounting the effective censorship that prohibits any large-scale debate about the legitimacy of the accepted property regimes. So let's grapple with the preconditions, both semiotic and material, of alternative information exchange—which ultimately means changing the current relations between the market, the state and the public domain or the commons. Without such a debate, aiming to create a program of substantive social transformation, what used to be called "the Left" will grow increasingly weaker, while the culture of privatization heightens world tensions by deepening basic inequalities. And that is reason enough for us to start right here. Beginning from the promise of free information exchange, one could develop three interlinked proposals:

1. The constitution of a cultural and informational commons, whose contents are freely usable and protected from privatization, using forms such as the General Public License for software (copyleft), the Creative Commons license for artistic and literary works, and the open-access journals for scientific and scholarly publications. This cultural and informational commons would run directly counter to WIPO/WTO treaties on intellectual property and would represent a clear alternative to the paradigm of cognitive capitalism, by conceiving human knowledge and expression as something essentially common, to be shared and made available as a virtual resource for future creation, both semiotic and embodied, material and immaterial.

2. The egalitarian transformation of existing, publicly funded cultural and scientific infrastructure (where elite interests determine the forms of mass consumption), through the invention of new forms and protocols of access to the means of the production and distribution of journalism, culture and scientific knowledge, and to the complex resources necessary for that production/distribution (archives, libraries, studio and rehearsal spaces, laboratories, university courses, etc.). This transformation—which alone can allow us to go beyond the domination of public-opinion formation by market-driven televisual media—would serve to encourage reasoned democratic debate (the exchange of ideas), but also autonomous artistic creation and expressive politics (social movements).

3. The re-invention of former programs of collective insurance safeguarding the health and well-being of society's members, but in a new and more diversified form, integrating both the demand for equality and the right to difference: guaranteed basic income, provision of low-priced lodging and basic services, health insurance and high-quality education for all. The challenge here is not to revive the bureaucratic state with its stultifying procedures of categorization and homogenization, but rather to invent new forms of appropriation and even of property, whose effects would be liberating but not isolating, socializing rather than narrowly individualizing.

Together, these proposals sketch the outlines of a far-reaching transformation. Yet each is simply essential for the concrete participation of citizens in an egalitarian democracy. For you cannot contribute to the wealth of global common goods without having access to the tools of production/distribution, and to existing informational and cultural resources; and yet this kind of engagement also requires that you have the time, time liberated from the relentless need to earn money for the basic necessities of social reproduction. The apparent audacity of ideas like the information commons or the guaranteed basic income—their apparent lack of "realism"—merely underscores the crying absence of the political in today's debates. There's more at stake here than a catchy tune, or a pill to make you dream. Only an ambition to change the rules of the economy and, ultimately, the existing form of the state, can supply the oppositional force that is needed in the early twentieth-first century. Yet the proposals above, inspired in part by the "digital revolution," indicate pragmatic changes which are already underway; they do not depend on electoral victories for their realization. Rather than a complete, finished program, they point toward an exodus from the present impasse. Semiotics with material consequences. Information-sharing to a very different tune.

Notes

1. "Berlin Declaration on Collectively Managed Online Rights: Compensation Without Control," at http://wizards-of-os.org/index.php?id=1699.
2. For a good description of the BOAI and links to corresponding initiatives, see the FAQ at http://www.earlham.edu/~peters/fos/boaifaq.htm#impactaffordable.
3. The information commons—a notion strongly influenced by the practice of open-source software distributed under the General Public License—is succinctly defined by Yochai Benkler in his article "The Political Economy of Commons," in *Upgrade*, June 2003, vol. IV, #3, available at www.upgrade-cepis.org/issues/2003/3/up4-3Benkler.pdf.
4. Source: *Libération*, July 8, 2004, at www.liberation.fr/page.php?Article=222215.
5. Text at www.wto.org/english/thewto_e/minist_e/min01_e/mindecl_trips_e.htm.
6. See the Health Global Access Project article at www.healthgap.org/press_releases/03/052103_HGAP_PS_WHA_US_IP.html.
7. "'Content Flatrate' and the Social Democracy of the Digital Commons," posted on Nettime on 13//7/04, at http://amsterdam.nettime.org/Lists-Archives/nettime-l-0407/msg00020.html.
8. M. Lazzarato, "Créer des mondes," in *Multitudes* 15 (Winter 2004), at http://multitudes.samizdat.net/article.php3?id_article=1285; the passage quoted figures in "Struggle, Event, Media" at www.republicart.net/disc/representations/lazzarato01_en.htm (translation modified).

9. Source: "Yale University Shares Profits From AIDS Drugs," *Le Monde diplomatique* Feb. 2002, available at www.mindfully.org/Industry/Yale-University-AIDS-ProfitsFeb02.htm.
10. "The Truth About the Drug Companies," *New York Review of Books*, vol. 51, # 12 (July 2004), available at www.nybooks.com/articles/17244.
11. Not only the free research, but also the extraordinarily high profitability of the manipulated US market excite the greed of European pharmaceutical corporations. See the references to the U.S. in the 2003 industry report of the European pharmaceutical lobby EFPIA, at www.efpia.org/6_publ/Infigures2003.pdf.
12. The relevant legislation is known as the Bayh–Dole act, passed in 1980 at the very outset of the neoliberal turn; text at www.cctec.cornell.edu/bayh-dole.html.
13. Source of these assertions: Eyal Press, Jennifer Washburn, "The Kept University," *The Atlantic* (March 2000).
14. Much of the writing in the French journal *Multitudes* has been devoted to the contradictions of "cognitive capitalism," which displaces the creation of surplus value into a largely semiotic realm—but to do so, relies on the intellectual and affective cooperation of people creating their own measures of value, and working outside any direct labor discipline. See esp. *Multitudes* 2 (May 2000), or the anthology *Vers un capitalisme cognitif* (Paris: L'Harmattan, 2001).

Forumaton, Barcelona 2004

14

EMANCIPATION

> *L'amour est la seule passion qui se paye
> d'une monnaie qu'elle fabrique elle-même.*
>
> Stendhal*

The "world market." Never have two words encompassed such promise. Power. Pleasure. Ubiquity. Freedom. And it's no illusion. The world market can get you that—if you obey its injunction. To distinguish yourself from the others. To stand apart. To rise above. To become the *sovereign individual*.

What is the paradox of the market individual?

To conform—through uniqueness and originality—to the perverse law of value which gives rarity its price. Within the world market, amidst the abundance of power, pleasure, ubiquity and freedom, each rare and precious individual has a price—on their head.

Let us consider what these statements might mean in the world of art today.

I

Among the paperback archives of vanished sciences is a 1971 work by Bertell Ollman, entitled *Alienation*. It is not, as you might suppose, a book that turns us away from a collective condition (workers' exploitation) toward an individual plight (the loss of one's authenticity, soul, or whatever). Because Ollman, in his interpretation of Marx, conceives of alienation as the severing of a social relation:

> The distortion in what Marx takes to be human nature is generally referred to in a language which suggests that an essential tie has been cut in the middle. Man is spoken of as being separated from his work (he plays no part in deciding what to do or how to do it)—a break between the individual and his life activity. Man is said to be separated from his own products (he has no control over what he makes or what becomes of it afterwards)—a break between the individual and the material world. He is also said to be separated from his fellow men (competition and class hostility have rendered most forms of cooperation impossible)—a break between man and man. In each instance, a relation that distinguishes the human species has disappeared and its constituent elements have been reorganized to appear as something else.[1]

If I look to the artists and cultural producers whom I respect and appreciate, it appears that Ollman has summed up everything most important to them. The decision as to what the artistic work will be, and how it will be carried out—and when, and where, and why—is not merely their individual choice, but it is never dictated from the outside. The desire for cooperation—and thus, for sharing the decision—has always been made into a substantial reality, either through the formation of groups, or through different kinds of temporary or long-term associations. The capacity to control, or at least, to remain responsible to the artistic products in their material circulation through society—and thus, the capacity to maintain the ethical basis of the project—is always a priority, resulting in elaborate mechanisms of presentation and distribution, principled conceptions (or rejections) of the rights to copy and authorship, and above all, a continuing concern for the extent and quality of use. None of these things should "appear as something else." The problem of alienation, in other words, has been taken seriously. Indeed the art, in these cases, is no longer an elaborately finished object arising from a unique inspiration; rather it is an ongoing process of relation which attends exactly to the questions of production, cooperation, responsibility. As though, even in the labyrinth of the most singular and intimate expression, what lay at stake were exactly what Marx and Ollman saw at risk in the relations of capitalist society: the sense of infinitely shared possibility "that distinguishes the human species."

Why is it so difficult to inscribe this possibility in contemporary institutions? Paolo Virno most persuasively develops this theme, in his discussions of the fundamentally linguistic form of work which he calls "virtuosity." He explains that three central functions which have traditionally been separate in the self-understanding of the Western societies, from Aristotle to Hannah Arendt, are now impossible to distinguish. These functions are labor, conceived as the productive expenditure of bodily energy; intellectual activity, which is silent and solitary; and political action, whose vector is public speech. But since the three have melded together with the advent of intellectual, affective and communicational forms of work—the so-called "immaterial labor" of the "general intellect"—Virno says that we virtuoso performers of the semiotic economy have come to live under a condition of infinite publicity without a public sphere. And the impossibility to make public meaning out of our performances —that is, the impossibility to shape a politics leading to concrete changes in society—is a humiliation of that which is at once the highest and most common of our faculties, namely the capacity of speech itself. The very capacity to articulate the infinite promise of our "species being" (Marx).[2]

The experience of transnational art exhibitions over the last fifteen years bears witness to this feeling of humiliation. Despite the continuing attraction of the events, no one is satisfied with the relations they have yielded—to say the least. In the catalogue of a recent "Yugoslav Biennial of Young Art," Mika Hannula describes this kind of exhibition as "the art of faking an orgasm." The title of Boris Buden's contribution is even more direct: "I don't want to be a Balkan in a subsidized biennial." Are such declarations a sign that the façade is finally cracking? Or just rumblings of discontent from the periphery? The institutional market for the arts expanded dramatically after the tumult of the late 1960s, when social-democratic governments suddenly felt compelled to buy off the new forms of expressive politics invented in the streets. It ballooned yet again after 1989, when European structural funds and globalized financial dividends were injected into a vastly expanded scene. But the cost of access to this fantastically enlarged production and distribution machinery is still the radical shrinkage of your symbolic ambitions to the level of cheap decor, or to the adolescent gestures of transgression, abstract denunciation, spectacular cynicism. All of which will serve as promotional material for foreign corporations and local politicians. The "institutional market"—where the general intellect stiffens into administration, or is spun off into saleable products, each with its personal signature—seems to occupy all the cultural space. And so in the world of art, despite admirable efforts, we have not yet surmounted what Marx and Ollman call "alienation."

Still, Virno's reflections add something to the picture. In fact they invert its terms, its figure/ground. For he is no longer talking about a stiuation in which the inherently emancipatory powers of art are blocked by archaic institutional structures, or damaged by the ferocity of the market. Instead what he describes is a productive machinery saturated with art, as though driven by the motor of invention. This is the postmodern economy, which generates surplus value on the basis of images and signs—while fabricating artificial rarities (and therefore class distinctions) from an initial situation of abundance (indeed, of infinite possibility). But how did this unbearable situation arise? What is the secret link that makes virtuosity, or artfulness itself, coincide so perfectly with publicity? That is, with the general form of communication, and indeed of subjectivation, in a market society?

II

The contemporary writer who has most effectively raised these questions is the Brazilian schizoanalyst Suely Rolnik. Her understanding of social relations begins from a phenomenology in which creative activity has a specific place. Our sensibility is divided, she explains, into perception and sensation: on the one hand, an empirical grasp of the world as form, leading to the establishment of fixed representations; on the other, an intensive encounter with the world as living force, which can be mobilized again in expressive activity. Empirical perception allows us to consolidate relatively stable maps of our situation in the world, but these constituted maps also act as an obstacle to the sensation of the constant irruption of otherness in our sensibility—and therefore to the creation of new modes of relation, which can only be effectively expressed through active resistance to the conservative forces shaped by the old schemas. From this outlook, we can conceive an agonistic involvement in the world, but one which does not only result in sterile confrontation with an objectified enemy; for political resistance itself is understood within the transformational dynamic of reknitting and even reinventing the relation with the other. Yet this expressive politics, which became widespread in the sixties and seventies, has been submitted over the last two decades to extremely sophisticated devices which split the force of creation from that of resistance. These devices (the specific forms of production in the postmodern economy) cause the creative process to turn nervously around its own axis, motivated by a capitalistically profitable, but existentially frustrating quest for the unattainable safe-havens of "luxury subjectivity," whose glossy image is continually projected by the media. In this reading, the prestigious exhibitions in which we compete to participate appear as simply another capture device for the force of invention (resulting in what Virno calls "servile virtuosity").[3]

Thus an economy based on the incessant production of images and signs is able to conjure up and expropriate a "wellspring of free invention power" — in a context where the word *freedom* has become a synonym of separation. In this situation, where each continually refines his or her originality in the endless, competitive quest to attain a higher personal price, it is not difficult to see how the "constituent elements" of a distinctively human relation have, in Ollman's terms, been reorganized "to appear as something else": the exercise of the productive force reappearing as a hunger for technological power; the ease of cooperative sociability reappearing as an egotistical thirst for pleasure; the sense of responsibility to the material complexity of society reappearing as a restless claim to ubiquity in the world-space. Suely Rolnik uses the figure of "perversion" to describe the way these distorted or twisted promises appear on the world market; and the word has the advantage of insisting on a dimension of subjective agency, even within a very large-scale productive apparatus like the communications media. But the urgency is surely to map out the specific social machines which carry out this reorganization of the human promise, and more, to describe their breakdown, to participate in their derailing, through activities which bring ourselves and our own position within the social arrangements into motion.

Opportunities for this kind of subversive mapping now exist, amidst tremendous change coupled with a mounting sense of frustration and disgust at the enduring status quo, even in the "luxury" realm of the art world. But who really makes this distinction of worlds anymore? The very extension of the market is erasing the differences, superimposing the maps, allowing for a clearer view of the basic processes at work. For example, the violent break-up of the Yugoslavian federation after a period of intense and often very positive cultural experimentation in the 1980s, and the authoritarian turn within its successor states, no longer appears so exceptional, so inexplicable. At a larger scale we can see that the tremendous ambivalence of the 1990s—by which I mean the violent deterritorialization of the capitalist globalization process, paralleled by the extraordinary freedom of communicational experimentation, the emergence all over the world of new social movements in the wake of the Zapatistas, and the first attempts at coordinated global struggles—has now given rise to exactly what the philosophical generation of the 1970s taught us to recognize and to flee: the "dialectical" return of the same, through the clash of seeming opposites. In this case, the return of neo-authoritarian American imperialism, in the face of a worldwide backlash against transnational neoliberalism—and the emergence of a regime of organized violence in which the "inner" and "outer" fronts continually intersect, resulting in a state of permanently episodic planetary civil war.[4] Of course, it may be difficult to accept that the modest practices of art have anything to do with such tremendous confrontations. But if we give up the specialized notion of art to recognize the wider role of "invention power" in the contemporary economy, then clearly what it produces has everything to do with the cultural conflicts in the world today.

III

Since the advent of democracy—and since Géricault's shockingly realistic studies of severed hands[5]—the question of going "beyond art" has been that of knitting a specialized, highly experimental and always threatened symbolic production back into the social body. Here is the secret link between politics, the avant-garde and healing, hidden in even the most alienated artistic representations (like the fantastic and depraved literature of William Burroughs). But never has there been a period so propitious for the deployment of this secret link as the present time, which has moved definitively beyond the avant-garde, to the extent that symbolic production has been taken up by broad sectors of the population. For this exact reason it has become much more crucial to understand the ways in which expression is made to turn around itself, in separation from its consequences in the world.

It is within this context that the art professionals wonder what to do with their museums, educational facilities and biennials. The question will not be answered so easily. Among the younger artists, at the "low end" or on the "periphery" of transnational circuits, the familiar image of improvised installations and deliberately schlock virtuosity—necessarily quick and cheap—will continually re-emerge as a kind of swallowed or half-muttered protest against "high-end" production values and the imposing displays of prestige that accompany them. Along the edges of this divide, the retreat into fine-arts nostalgia—or conceptual overkill—will remain classic, repetitive escapes. But in reality all that is obsolete today. The urgency is to express the paths of new cartographies, which transversally link artists, social movements, civil-society initiatives, knowledge-production centers and media technologies, always across the major center-periphery divides (whether these are encountered at urban, national, or transnational levels). And it would clearly be useful if many more people—across the spectrums from "high" to "low," from "center" to "periphery"—would openly proclaim the current impasse, and begin to take the risks of transformation.

For many people, the mere existence of transnational art circuits represents a rare and important chance to participate in the flux of exchange that is the very essence of social life in the early twentieth-first century. But that chance is not reason enough to make humanity itself into a rarity. Or to put an alienated price on your own head. The creation of new social machines begins with the power of exodus, in a kind of passion that "pays for itself in a currency of its own fabrication," as Stendhal wrote so beautifully. But to reassert an expressive politics, and in this way, to invent a new form of public life, more adequate to the complex demands of the present, but also more able to liberate the abundance of the human promise, seems to me the real challenge of our time. And this is a contemporary meaning for the word "emancipation."

Notes

* "Love is the only passion that pays for itself in a currency of its own fabrication."
1 Bertell Ollman, *Alienation: Marx's Conception of Man in Capitalist Society* (New York: Cambridge University Press, 1971), pp. 133–34.
2 Virno also speaks, more precisely, of "the general aptitudes of the mind: the faculty of language, the disposition to learn, the capacity for abstraction and relation, access to self-reflection." Cf. Paolo Virno, "Virtuosité et révolution," in *Miracle, virtuosité et déja-vu: trois essais sur l'idée du monde* (Paris: L'Eclat, 1996); on line at . The virtuoso's humiliation within infinite publicity was discussed in his lecture in at the MacBa in Barcelona, Dec. 1, 2003.
3 See, among many others, Suely Rolnik, "Creation Quits its Pimp, To Rejoin Resistance," in *Zehar* 51, 2003. Rolnik's texts can be accessed at www.u-tangente.org.
4 Cf. Philippe Zarifian, "Pourquoi ce nouveau régime de guerre?", *Multitudes* 11 (Winter 2003), pp. 11–23.
5 Gericault, *Study of Truncated Limbs*, ca. 1818–19, Musée Fabre, Montpellier; image online at www.tate.org.uk/britain/exhibitions/constabletodelacroix/room2.htm. Also see Chris Marker's film on the worldwide revolutions of 1968, *Grin without a Cat* (1977), part I, "Fragile Hands," part II, "Severed Hands."

15

REVERSE IMAGINEERING

TOWARD THE NEW URBAN STRUGGLES, OR, WHY SMASH THE STATE WHEN YOUR NEIGHBORHOOD THEME-PARK IS SO MUCH CLOSER?

> What are the steps in the creation of a Disney attraction? According to literature sent out by WDW [Walt Disney World], the steps are: storyboard, script, concept, show models, sculpture, show set design, graphics, interiors, architectural design, molds and casting, wardrobe and figure finishing, electronic and mechanical design and manufacture, show sets and prop construction, animation, audio, special effects and lighting, and engineering. — *The Unofficial Walt Disney Imagineering Page* (www.imagineering.org).

On October 17, 2003, seven groups of some 20 to 30 persons descended into the Paris metro, with paint pots, glue, rollers, brushes, spray cans, sheets of paper and marking pens in their hands. Their aim? To overwrite, cover up, deface, subvert, recompose or simply rip to shreds as many advertisements as possible, without violence to any individual or to any piece of property, other than the images which impinge on our most intimate desires. Arising against a background of aggressive cuts in public programs which had originally been designed to withdraw specific activities and times of life from market pressures—cuts which affect teachers, the unemployed, retirees, researchers and performing artists, among others—the "stopub" movement declared its intention: "to attack the driving force of this commodification: advertising. It invades our public space, the streets, the subways, the TV. It's everywhere, on our clothes, our walls, our screens. Let's resist it, with creative, peaceful and legitimate means." And resist it they did, organizing three more major actions in the metro before the end of the year, defacing over 9,000 advertisements and causing almost a million euros of "damage"—at least from the viewpoint of the organization charged with selling the display space, or more precisely, the psychic space of millions of people who ride the trains every day.[1]

The French "stop advertising" campaigns in the fall of 2003 would have been unimaginable without a previous event: the cancellation of the Avignon summer theater festival under the pressure of strikes by part-time performing-arts and audiovisual workers. This movement includes actors, stage directors, set designers, decorators, dancers, choreographers, tightrope walkers, fire breathers, clowns and jugglers, sound and lighting technicians, costume makers, film directors and editors, gaffers, cameramen and women, best boys, location managers, dubbers, special effects creators, animation designers and innumerable other professionals: all the people whose job it is to create imaginary worlds. Since 1969, these *"intermittents du spectacle"* had gained the right to a specific form of unemployment insurance which recognized the inherent discontinuities of artistic practice, and provided a supplemental income to cover the periods when paid labor gives way to volunteer productions, rehearsals, training periods, the quest for inspiration or the search for another contract. But in June of 2003, the agreement governing this form of unemployment insurance was abruptly modified by the French employers' organization and three minority unions, in an attempt to eliminate roughly 30% of the beneficiaries.[2] The *intermit-*

tents responded with detailed proposals to reform the law, but also with a seemingly endless stream of protest actions, mounting counter-performances all over France, occupying government buildings and interrupting ministerial speeches, creating films, organizing debates, and using their special knowledge to break into national TV programs and take over the mike during live broadcasts. Perhaps the most impressive of these break-ins was the disruption of the reality show "Star Academy," where the part-time theater workers surged onto the set and unfurled a banner reading "Shut Off Your TVs"—symbolically attacking what is literally a training ground for the professional fetishes of the spectacle society.

Around the same time, a much broader social movement was forming: the self-organization of casual or "precarious" labor. The catalyst was a group of Italian activists based in Milan, who called themselves the Chainworkers. Using the simplest of visual and rhetorical tools, they built an iconic language that could reach out simultaneously to kids doing chain-store jobs, temp-service workers, and freelance professionals—the so-called cognitariat, who are sometimes better paid than the others, but face similarly uncertain conditions. To begin organizing they did illegal demonstrations and banner-drops inside shopping malls where all rights to assembly in public are curtailed. Their website, chainworkers.org, was conceived as an information resource and a way to create collective consciousness. But their best tactic proved to be the reinvention of the traditional Mayday demonstration, around the theme of precarious labor conditions. By 2003, the event had already outstripped anything the unions could muster: the next year it brought together 50,000 people in Milan and had spread to Barcelona; in 2005 it took place in twenty different European cities. Conscious of the way that the consumption environments of the postmodern metropolis play constantly on our desires and emotions, the new labor organizers have made Mayday into a subversive fashion parade, where the technicians of the commodity culture use their on-the-job skills to act out an expressive reversal of their ordinary alienation. Instead of opposing the spectacular image, as previous generations did, they aim to pirate it, appropriate it, recreate it on a different basis and for different ends.

What's behind these new protest movements, which take the urban stage as their own living room, or as their own multimedia studio? Can these gestures of revolt be situated in a socio-economic context? Writing in the early 1970s on *The Urban Question*, the sociologist Manuel Castells conceived the city, not as a directly productive machine, but instead as the realm of "collective consumption."[3] The facilities of the city were furnished by the state in order to ensure the reproduction of the working class, according to the needs of capital. For Castells, urban movements demanding improvements and amenities—that is to say, use values—represented a displacement of the basic struggle between the proletariat and the bourgeoisie. Every new housing project, sports field or cultural center was a victory for the oppressed, at a cost that would someday break the backs of the owners. Such a sociological schema seems far away today, when the demands for collective facilities have faded, amidst the rise of a more "flexible" economy. The city now appears as a realm where consumption is imposed upon the individual. To succeed in doing so, a special environment must be created for the tastes of every target group. The theorist Maurizio Lazzarato has written of the way that corporations "create worlds" to seduce their consumers and producers.[4] City councils, development agencies and heritage departments also "create worlds," in the service of local and international businesses. Urban real estate is conceived as a piece of productive equipment, even, or especially, when it is being used for amusement. The leisure worlds of postmodern cities are very profitable for their owners. But no one dares to say that their consumers—or even worse, their producers—might find them revolting to the taste. Which is also a way of denying that the new movements are truly political.

What kind of imaginary worlds do we want to live in? And how do we want to pay for them? At the outset of the twenty-first century, on a planet at war, one of the rising conflicts in the overdeveloped countries revolves around what some call culture, and others, entertainment. What we begin to see are struggles *within* what the Situationists termed "the spectacle."[5] At stake are the human creations which make up our everyday environment: the fictional narratives and perceptual stimulations which, like other forms of knowledge, can be conceived either as common goods or as saleable commodities. The theater of the new struggles is the so-called "creative city." Its managers now propose constant improvements, infinite amenities, in a race to keep up with the theme-parks that are constantly being built in the suburbs. But the stars that are being painted above our heads—with the help of transnational corporations—deserve to be met with an alternative vision, an antagonistic cosmology. It is a matter of bringing the stars back down to human level, of dissolving the commercial mythologies. It is a matter of assembling what Deleuze and Guattari call a "nomadic war machine," to subversively deconstruct the imaginary environment that transnational state capitalism is constructing.[6] What follows are the elements of the struggle to recreate the world-city.

EARTH

The ground of the new urban struggles began to take form some three to four decades ago, in the wake of changes in class composition that first became apparent in the overdeveloped countries in the late 1960s. Mass education was one aspect of these changes, as important fractions of the former working classes gained access to socialized universities. In the early 1970s, Alexander Kluge and Oscar Negt pointed out that research and education formed a major contradiction in the planned economy: because innovation is centrally necessary to a technological society, but it is also rare and largely unpredictable, requiring vast investments in a wide variety of disciplines, without any certain results in the output of each individual student or teacher.[7] Thus, all kinds of autonomous investigations could proliferate freely in the state-subsidized educational institutions, independently of any market regulation. Experiments with pure use values, withdrawn from the constraints of monetary exchange, were accompanied by calls for even greater entitlements; and state-funded theorists went so far as to imagine a post-capitalist society. To this development of mass intellectuality must be added what the Italian autonomists have termed "the refusal of work": a widespread rejection of the alienating conditions of factory labor, ultimately leading to the decline of large-scale, labor-intensive manufacturing processes in the old industrial centers, and to the exodus of workers from the direct control of managerial hierarchies.[8] The industrial discipline of the postwar societies began to dissolve into a broad spectrum of radical-democratic demands for emancipation.

The conception, and even more, the *use* of the modern city were gradually altered by this double dynamics of mass intellectuality and the refusal of hierarchical structures. Consider a characteristic formulation of 1960s counter-urbanism: Henri Lefebvre's *The Right to the City*, written with the explicit aim to "break up systems," to undermine rationalized specialization and class segregation. Lefebvre does not see the city as a reproduction machine, a marketplace or decision-making center, but rather as an enduring *artwork* to be freely appropriated: "The city is itself *'oeuvre,'* a feature which contrasts with the irreversible tendency towards money and commerce, towards exchange and *products*. Indeed, the *oeuvre* is use value and the product is exchange value. The eminent use of the city, that is, of its streets and squares, edifices and monuments, is *la Fête* (a celebration which consumes unproductively...)."[9] Lefebvre envisioned an urban theater of mobile centers, conjured up and dissolved at will by the city-dwellers' appropriation of their immediate environment. The aesthete will recognize the links to Huizinga's figure of *homo ludens*, to the nomadic designs of Constant or Archigram, to the playful, labyrinthine architecture of Aldo van Eyck—while the activist recalls the Situationist *dérive* and the "constructed situation," or the revolutionary theatrics of the Provos in Holland and the Diggers in America. All of these interventions sought to open up the modernist city to the "eminent use" of the popular *fête*. Yet isn't the urban theme park of today just such a festival environment? What were the consequences of the aesthetic politics of the sixties?

To understand how Situationist-type aesthetics combined with a changing class composition to produce a long-term transformation of metropolitan culture, we will need a reference to a very different model of artistic activity in the mid-1960s: Andy Warhol's "Factory" in New York. Against a backdrop of industrial decay, the artist-impresario opened the doors of an archaic manufacturing building to a gallery of marginal figures—drifters, drug users, transvestites, gays and lesbians, bohemians escaping their class origins—who would experiment with photography, film, television, musical styles (The Velvet Underground), but also with transgressive parties, hedonistic excess. These fringe subjectivities, the exotic detritus of ordinary life, were the "superstars" of the Factory; but only Warhol, with his media aura, could successfully play the role of Hollywood producer and bring them the distribution that they all craved (their "fifteen minutes of fame"). Out of this voluntary blurring of the classes in the post-industrial Factory there emerged two key innovations: the first was a new model of subcultural production, freely translating the energies of social mobility and class conflict into hybrid media commodities; and the second was a new aesthetic of urban inhabitation, based on the gritty attractions of "transitional neighborhoods." Subcultural production, exploiting all the immediacy of the garage band and the home studio, would become an integral part of the postmodern economy identified by Frederic Jameson;[10] while the aesthetics of the urban margins would play a leading role in the speculative renovation of the former industrial areas of modern cities (gentrification).[11] This relation between subcultural production and real-estate speculation, which only became obvious in Europe in the 1980s,[12] is what has laid the ambiguous ground of today's urban struggles.

(HOT) AIR

How can youth energies be captured, transgressive desires satisfied and egalitarian claims laid to rest, despite the ongoing progress of segregation and homogenization? How can mass intellectuality be captured and channeled, made productive in the cultural-informational economy, without too much political conflict over the content of what is produced? The consensus-building functions of the postmodern economy's "cultural turn" should never be minimized. The compromise-formation of subcultural production acts to absorb the energies of class mobility, stabilizing them in multimedia proximity to the hard data of the financial sector. Spatially you see similar outcomes: the computer-assisted service industries scattered throughout the renovated manufacturing zones, the edge-city clubs and bar scenes located within prowling range of the glittering business districts. Cultural and subcultural production—of media, fashion, live performance and urban space itself—become important assets for metropolitan rivalry, as cities with global pretensions compete to attract businesses, tourists and talent. Today, the "creative city," and even the "creative class," are the buzzwords of urban development.[13] Against this background, it is hard to disagree with Eve Chiapello and Luc Boltanski's contention that the "artistic critique" of the 1960s has furnished a set of values and attitudes that can easily be exploited for the networked business strategies.[14] And these strategies in turn become the coveted object of urban governance.

The case in point is Barcelona. The ten-year strategic plan for the city's cultural sector explicitly aims to "strengthen Barcelona as a factory that produces cultural contents," to "make culture a key element of social cohesion," to "incorporate Barcelona into the flows of digital culture" and to "project Barcelona as a platform of international promotion."[15] Recognizing the specific characteristics of networked social structure as described by native son Manuel Castells—ironically enough, since Castells had been the prophet of urban struggles in 1970s—the strategic plan of the Catalan capital outlines "a new management model for culture," based on contractual agreements or "pacts" rather than strictly hierarchical relations between actors, acknowledging the need for autonomy in the development and progressive adaptation of projects to changing situations, and proposing evaluation techniques for the "follow-up" (read: control) "of the cultural pulse of a specific territory (the evolution of cultural practices, the economic dimension of cultural activity, the analysis of the impact of culture in the economic and social context, the analysis of creation, etc.)." This cultural/economic planning appears as the public-sector equivalent of what is known in business circles as "knowledge management."[16] But can the creative class or "cognitariat" be successfully controlled? And what happens to the subversive dynamics of transgressive mobility and social cooperation?

In Europe, the British government has most deliberately developed the planning of pop-cultural production, with an explicit concern for the future of the new labor force that was reflected in the culture ministry's publication of the "Creative Industries Mapping Document" in 2001. This policy text attempts to delineate a bewildering range of new professions: Arts Promoter, Incubator, Consultancy for Inventor, Cultural Strategist, Multimedia Artist, Visual Support Consultant, Media Initiatives and Relations, Digital Design Consultant, Branding and Communications, New Media Agent, Bio-Entrepreneur (!), etc.[17] The attempt to functionalize the so-called creative industries emerged against the background of the "Young British Art" in the mid-nineties, driven by the advertising magnate Saatchi and accompanied by the media froth generated around the slogan "Cool Britannia" in the years 1996–98, with the publication of the book *Creative Britain* by Culture Minister Chris Smith in 1998 and Tony Blair's highly conspicuous flirting with the pop-star milieus—all concurrent with the massification of the Internet and the emergence of so-called "new media." But the drafting of the mapping document also follows after a long period of high unemployment and casualization of the labor market brought on by two decades of neoliberal policy, as well as a serious recession in the early 1990s which saw a fresh influx of marginal cultural producers to London, to occupy spaces temporarily abandoned by capital.[18] The dream of integrating a whole wave of new arrivals to the labor market via highly individualized career-paths articulated around the promise of creative autonomy and the productive tools of the latest technology may now sound rather unlikely, after the krach of the "new economy" and the dramatic rise in social tensions all across the planet in the wake of September 11. Yet the formula of the creative city is still being sold by high-level consultancies[19] to municipal planning departments across the overdeveloped world, with the eager approbation of local and transnational corporations—perpetually obsessed with the rebranding of everything, even the city itself, for global consumption.

FIRE

In the artistic fields delivered over to neoliberal management, as in corporate funded-research, the emphasis falls invariably on immediately marketable skills and products—an emphasis which continually raises the levels of frustration, even at the heart of the well-paid cognitariat. Freelance labor, initially promoted as an emancipation from hierarchy, soon reveals its price in subtle or blatant forms of surveillance through mobile communications devices, introjecting professional responsibilities into every hour of the day, into every living space and personal relation.[20] Meanwhile, relentless increases in ground rent restrict access to the city, while mounting police pressure (modeled on New York Mayor Giuliani's "zero tolerance") is applied to any kind of deviant behavior. The danger of "slipping through the cracks" in societies which have abandoned their welfare safety nets can now be felt throughout the casualized labor force. Yet at the same time, even the most basic jobs increasingly call for "facework," spontaneity, affective presence, intelligence, creativity. Ours is the age of what the German labor ministry has called the *Ich-AG*, the "I-corporation." Biopower, in contemporary capitalism, means turning the self into a business. The subjective consequences of the knowledge economy include a new blurring of the personal/the economic/the political, pushing a resurgent counter-culture to respond by experimenting with models of free cooperation and temporary autonomous zones. And so biopower gives rise to biopolitics: "When self-exploitation acquires a central function in the process of valorization, the production of subjectivity becomes a terrain of central conflict," remarks labor specialist and leftist philosopher André Gorz. "Social relations withdrawn from the grip of value, from competitive individualism and market exchange, make the latter appear by contrast in their political dimension, as extensions of the power of capital. A front of total resistance opens up. It necessarily overflows the domain of knowledge production toward new ways of living, of consuming, of collectively appropriating public space and everyday culture. Reclaim the Streets is one of its most successful expressions."[21]

The cycle of antiglobalization protests, launched in the overdeveloped countries by the European wing of the Peoples Global Action network in 1998, constituted the first eruption of this "front of total resistance" on the networked urban territory of the world-cities. Marked by a confluence of traditional social movements, single-issue activist groups, disaffected urban youth and rebellious cultural producers—visual and performance artists, musicians, open-air DJs, media freaks and computer hackers—these demonstrations often take the form of politically oriented techno-parties, no longer simply eluding police repression, but using all the resources of cooperative cultural production to actively target the sites and symbols of corporate control over intimate consciousness and public expression.[22] If Seattle brought this front of resistance to a higher level, it was not only because of the greater complexity of the social movements involved, nor only because of the direct influence that the movement could now claim over decision-making at the summit. It was also because of the intensity of the urban battle, sparked off by disciplined affinity groups using sophisticated techniques of civil disobedience, and pursued by anarchist "Black Blocs" and untold numbers of city-dwellers revolted by the violence of what one analyst called a "police riot."[23] A Niketown sales outlet, epitomizing the exploitation of distant labor, the cooptation of subcultural creativity and the transformation of the city into a corporate theme-park, was deliberately attacked and destroyed, giving rise in the process both to a transnational urban legend and to a complex form of solidarity between the social classes. Similar demonstrations took place in Washington D.C., Sydney, Prague, Nice, Seoul, Quebec City, Barcelona, Göteburg and other metropolitan centers, accompanied by the development of the Indymedia network and a process of intensive translocal exchange. For many in Europe, the movement came to a head in July of 2001 in Genoa, with a police riot on the scale of the one in Seattle and the murder of a protestor, Carlo Giuliani, followed soon after by the paralyzing shock of September 11. But a giant step further was taken in the highly developed but peripheral country of Argentina, where a currency crisis brought about an alliance between unemployed workers and the middle class, toppling the government with massive demonstrations on December 19 and 20, 2001, and opening a year-long period of radical social experimentation.

WATER

Today, the Argentine movement fallen, and the counterglobalization demonstrations have been pushed by terror and Imperial warfare into the background of mediated consciousness. But the urban knowledge engendered during this cycle of struggles has given rise to a vast network of subversive potential, which permeates the breadth and depth of the world-cities. The autonomous marxist Harry Cleaver likens contemporary rhizomatic or meshworked social movements to the flux of what he calls the *hydrosphere*: "oceans with their ever restless currents and eddies, now moving faster, now slower, now warmer, now colder, now deeper, now on the surface."[24] The intermingling currents which have begun to change class composition on a planetary scale[25] convey both an intense awareness of the ways in which intimate desire can be manipulated, and a willingness to intervene in the creation of imaginary worlds. In this context, artists have regained a political protagonism. An example is the project "Nike Ground—Rethinking Space," by 0100101110101101.org. Expanding on the corporate-chameleon strategies of ®™ark and the Yes Men,[26] this group collaborated with the alternative cultural center Public Netbase to illegally set up a 13-ton "infobox" on the Karlsplatz in Vienna. The imposing, glass-walled container distributed an enthusiastic and bizarrely serious proposal to rename the historic square "Nikeplatz" and to install a gigantic red "swoosh" sculpture at its center. One of the texts reads: *"Picture this: rethinking space. Having the chance to redesign the city where you live... It's Nike Ground! This revolutionary project is transforming and updating your urban space. Nike is introducing its legendary brand into squares, streets, parks and boulevards: Nikesquare, Nikestreet, Piazzanike, Plazanike or Nikestrasse will appear in major world capitals over the coming years..."*[27] Residents were outraged at the project, and a furor arose in the press; Nike threatened legal action, then finally withdrew all charges. As a 01001 spokeswoman explained: "For this work, we wanted to use the entire city as a stage for a huge urban performance, a sort of theatre show for an unaware audience/cast. We wanted to produce a collective hallucination capable of altering people's perception of the city in this total, immersive way."[28]

Can the sophisticated programs of corporate and municipal imagineering be challenged or even undone by a "long wave" of subversive projects, operating at different scales and temporalities, intersecting with the sudden outbursts of generalized urban struggles? Reverse engineering, as a hackers' manual explains, "is simply the act of figuring out what software that you have no source code for does in a particular feature or function, to the degree that you can either modify this code, or reproduce it in another independent work."[29] The conceptual group Bureau d'Ètudes extends the principle to sociopolitical dimensions: "The deconstruction of complex machines and their 'decolonized' reconstruction can be carried out on all kinds of objects, not just computational ones. In the same way as you deconstruct a program, you can also deconstruct the internal functioning of a government or an administration, a firm or an industrial or financial group. On the basis of such a deconstruction, involving a precise identification of the operating principles of a given administration, or the links or networks between administrations, lobbies, businesses etc., you can define modes of action or intervention."[30] Beyond virtuoso stunts like "Nike Ground," one can see the tactics of the emerging social movements—such as the "stop publicity" campaign or the *intermittents du spectacle* in France—as attempts to precisely deconstruct the neoliberal program of total social mobilization for the needs of a flexible economy. These tactics receive widespread support from the cultural/educational sectors, where there is an increasing awareness of the way that all "free time" is being subordinated to market calculations. An expanding range of professionals and self-taught experts are turning their autonomous energies—their "off hours," if you prefer—to urban subversion. But can such efforts avoid the social and economic capture-devices which tend to isolate a relatively privileged "cognitariat" from the rest of the casualized labor force, or indeed, from the rest of the population? The Chainworkers group has sought to answer that question, by involving the widest social spectrum possible in the new-style Mayday parades. And the *intermittents*, uncomfortably conscious of the relative privilege afforded by their unique form of unemployment insurance, conclude their texts and speeches with this phrase: "What we defend, we defend for everyone."

The struggle over the definition of social services, scientific research, cultural production and the natural and built environments either as private commodities or as common goods under some form of collective stewardship has become one of the central conflicts of our time, disputed on a territory that extends from intimate subjectivities to the networked spaces of politics.[31] Given the manipulability of public opinion in the contemporary media democracies, the destinies of this struggle will depend crucially on people's ability to recognize and resist the new techniques of social management. In this regard, some interesting news has come from one of the premier "creative cities," Barcelona. Spurred on by the successful instrumentalization of the Olympic Games in 1992, construction and real-estate interests again joined hands with the city government in the mid-1990s to plan an urban infotainment project: "Forum 2004," also known as the "Universal Forum of Cultures." Held in a vast new seaside facility built right next to the poorest district in the metropolitan region (but without any particular benefit for that district), this 3 billion-euro project could act not only as a tourist magnet and an immense source of revenue for construction companies, but also as a simulacrum of the contemporary Social Forum movement, conducted under the direct control of the municipality and its corporate backers. Thus the manufacture of consensus is revealed as the primary postmodern industry: "The Forum does not claim to maintain an equal distance between Davos and Puerto Alegre, but to be the meeting place of the two poles, an exercise of dialogue between opposites," wrote the director of the event.[32] But what does such a meeting lead to in reality?

A few days before that declaration was published, a conference had been convened in a public meeting hall, the Ateneu Barcelonés, under the title "Fòrum 2004: la gran impostura." Speakers claimed that the forum was "something more than a lie and a fake"—it was "an expression of the new political management of life" designed to "promote the trademark of Barcelona."[33] Beyond all expectations, the hall was packed to overflowing. A broad, heterogeneous "Assembly of Resistances" began to plan collective actions of various kinds, in order to expose and discredit the Barcelona model of speculative city planning.[34] Architects, artists, filmmakers, philosophers, economists, urbanists, political activists, ecologists and squatters all resolved to begin deconstructing the spectacular machinery. One ephemeral collective that came to be known as "Mapas"[35] undertook a detailed cartography of the "precarious city," showing the sponsorship links between the Forum and temporary employment services, consumer-product distributors, arms dealers, polluting industries, etc., and indicating the precise location of their corporate offices on a folding map which was printed massively and given away at every occasion. The idea was to produce a threatening atmosphere, then bifurcate in unexpected directions. An action was undertaken against the arms manufacturer Indra, which was to provide communications systems for the festival of peace: several dozen white-suited "civil inspectors" surged up the stairway of the firm's Barcelona office and began dismantling the telephones and computers, which were placed into boxes marked "Danger: Weapons of Mass Destruction."

But the Indra action was only the beginning of the counter-spectacles against the Forum. Even more effectively, a photographic Forumaton was set up in various locations, allowing snickering residents to "pose against the Forum," with signs that said "The Forum is a business," "The Forum is for real-estate speculation," "The Forum is a piece of shit," "The Forum is precarity," and so on.[36] These pictures were circulated through the web; but they were also picked up by the local papers, and an undercurrent of laughter began to accompany the omnipresent publicity of the event. Finally a crescendo was hit with *Pateras Urbanas*, an invasion of the Forum by land, air and sea—with marching protestors, a hang glider, and above all a fleet of precarious rafts, recalling those used by immigrants crossing the Straits of Gibralter.[37] The construction of the rafts turned into a surprisingly popular attraction. Hundreds of participants; outlandish costumes, pirate flags; four hours in the ocean with the Coast Guard everywhere; and a wild landing on the grounds of the tourist spectacle that wanted to turn its back on anything real. As though the long wave of subversive projects had already begun washing over the neoliberal city...

Jan. 2004/May 2005

Notes

1. For information on the movement, see www.actionstopub.tk and http://bap.propagande.org, as well as André Gattolin, Thierry Lefebvre, "Stopub: analyse provisoire d'un rhizome activiste," in *Multitudes* 16 (Spring 2004), available at http://multitudes.samizdat.net/article.php3?id_article=1376.
2. Cf. http://cip-idf.ouvaton.org, as well as *Multitudes* 17, dossier on "L'intermittence dans tous ses états" (Summer 2004).

3. See *The Urban Question: A Marxist Approach* (Cambridge, Mass.: MIT, 1977; 1st ed. 1972).
4. Maurizio Lazzarato, *Les révolutions du capitalisme* (Paris: Les Empêcheurs de penser en rond, 2004), chap. 3; an initial version of this argument can be found in "Créer des mondes," *Multitudes* 15 (Winter 2004), at http://multitudes.samizdat.net/article.php3?id_article=1285.
5. With respect to the strike of the intermittants, Jean Baudrillard speaks of a "just revenge against the spectacle—by the spectacle-makers themselves." In "Les Suicidés du spectacle," *Libération*, July 16, 2003, archived at: http://library.nothingness.org/articles/SI/fr/display/370.
6. Gilles Deleuze, Félix Guattari, "Treatise on Nomadology—The War Machine" in *A Thousand Plateaus: Capitalism and Schizophrenia* (U. Minn. Press, 1987; 1st ed. 1980).
7. Alexander Kluge, Oscar Negt, *Public Sphere and Experience* (U. Minn. Press, 1993; 1st ed. 1972).
8. Antonio Negri, *Marx Beyond Marx* (New York: Autonomedia, 1991; 1st ed. 1979); also see Negri's essay in *Des entreprises pas comme les autres: Benetton en Italie et Le Sentier à Paris* (Publisud, 1993).
9. Henri Lefebvre, "The Right to the City," in *Writings on Cities* (Oxford: Blackwell, 1996; 1st ed. 1968).
10. Frederic Jameson, *Postmodernism, or, The Cultural Logic of Late Capitalism* (Verso, 1991; original article 1984), at http://xroads.virginia.edu/~DRBR/JAMESON/jameson.html.
11. Sharon Zukin, *Loft Living: Culture and Capital in Urban Change* (Rutgers University Press, New Brunswick N.J.: 1989; 1st ed. 1982).
12. For a case study of urban transformation and subculture politics in the 1980s, Christian Schmid, "The Dialectics of Urbanisation in Zurich," in INURA (eds.), *Possible Urban Worlds* (Basel: Birkhäuser Verlag, 1998).
13. Charles Landry, *The Creative City: A Toolkit for Urban Innovators* (London: Earthscan, 2000); Richard Florida, *The Rise of the Creative Class* (New York: Basic Books, 2002); Paul Ray, Sherry Anderson, *The Cultural Creatives* (New York: Three Rivers Press, 2000).
14. Luc Boltanski, Eve Chiapello, *Le Nouvel esprit du capitalisme* (Paris: Gallimard, 1999); English summary at www.sociologia.unimib.it/mastersqs/rivi/boltan.pdf.

15. "Strategic Plan of the Cultural Sector of Barcelona," at www.bcn.es/accentcultura/angl.
16. For an example of the knowledge-management business, see www.debonothinkingsystems.com.
17. Department for Culture, Media and Sport, "Creative Industries Mapping Document," at: www.culture.gov.uk/global/publications/archive_2001/ci_mapping_doc_2001.htm; cf. Angela McRobbie, "'Everyone is Creative,'" at www.k3000.ch/becreative/texts/text_5.html.
18. For gentrification in the Hackney district of London, see the texts and videos by The London Particular, at http://thelondonparticular.org. For a view from inside the machinery of gentirification, Emma Dexter, "Picturing the City," in *Century City: Art and Culture in the Modern Metropolis*, exhib. cat., Tate Modern, London, Feb. 1 - April 29, 2001; and for critique of the art-advertising-urban development complex, Julian Stallabrass, *High Art Lite* (London: Verso, 1999), as well as my article "Reflecting Museums," at www.u-tangente.org.
19. Cf. the list of consultancies in *Creative Cities*, op. cit.
20. Cf. Philippe Zarifian, "Les sociétés de contrôle," in *A quoi sert le travail?* (Paris: La Dispute, 2003), as well as Brian Holmes, "The Flexible Personality," at www.u-tangente.org.
21. Interview with André Gorz, "Economie de la connaissance, exploitation des savoirs," in *Multitudes* 15 (Winter 2004).
22. Cf. "Friday June 18th 1999," in *Do or Die* 8, at www.ecoaction.org/dod/no8/j18.html.
23. Cf. Paul de Armond, "Netwar in the Emerald City," at http://nwcitizen.com/publicgood/reports/wto.
24. Cf. www.rtmark.com, www.theyesmen.org.
25. Harry Cleaver, "Computer-linked Social Movements and the Global Threat to Capitalism," downloadable at www.cseweb.org.uk/downloads/cleaver.pdf.
26. For an idea of the class composition, cf. Notes from Nowhere collective (eds.), *We Are Everywhere: The Irresistible Rise of Global Anticapitalism* (London: Verso, 2003), website at www.weareeverywhere.org.
27. "Nike Ground—Rethinking Space," at www.nikeground.com.

28. "Nike Buys Streets and Squares," at http://0100101110101101.ORG/home/nikeground/story.html.
29. Mike Perry, Nasko Oskov, "Introduction to Reverse Engineering Software," at www.acm.uiuc.edu/sigmil/RevEng/.
30. Bureau d'Ètudes, "Autonomous Knowledge and Power in a Society without Affects," at www.u-tangente.org.
31. On common goods, cf. Philippe Aigrain, "Pick the Right Modernity," downloadable at http://www.debatpublic.net/ Members/paigrain/texts/bienscommuns.pdf (in French at www.debatpublic.net/Members/paigrain/texts/bienscommuns.pdf).
32. "El Fòrum quiere ser el punto de encuentro de Davos con Porto Alegre," in *El País*, supplement "Cultura," Jan. 25, 2004.
33. "Los grupos críticos con el 2004 reúnen mil personas en el Ateneu," in *La Vanguardia*, Jan. 22, 2004.
34. See www.moviments.net/resistencies2004.
35. See www.sindominio.net/mapas. A short film of the Indra intervention, described below, can be found in the "action" section of this site, at the bottom of the page.
36. See www.sindominio.net/mapas/forumaton/forumaton_home.htm.
37. See www.paterasurbanas.net.

16

TRANSPARENCY & EXODUS

POLITICAL PROCESS
IN THE MEDIATED DEMOCRACIES

> What is it that separates the left from the right?... Fundamentally, it is nothing but a processual calling, a *processual passion*.
>
> Félix Guattari[1]

In October of 1968, in Rosario, Argentina, the artist Graciela Carnevale invited visitors to what would be the final opening of a "Cycle of Experimental Art" held in a storefront space in the city. Her contribution to the series consisted in luring the public inside, then slipping out to lock the door and enclose the crowd within the gallery. The visitors became the material of a social artwork. The question was: How would they react to this imprisonment? Who would finally shatter the glass to release the captives from the trap? "Through an act of aggression, the work tends to provoke the spectator to a heightened consciousness of the power whereby violence is exerted in the everyday world," wrote the artist. "On a daily basis we passively submit, through fear, connivance and complicity, to all the degrees of violence, from the most subtle and degrading violence that coerces our thinking via communications media broadcasting false contents provided by their owners, to the most provocative and scandalous violence exerted on a student's life."[2] In the event, the public submitted. After an hour, the blow that finally shattered the glass came from outside. A photograph shows a woman crouching down to exit through a jagged hole in the window.

At the same time, Graciela Carnevale was also part of the project known as *Tucumán Arde*, or "Tucumán is Burning"—an experimental process of information analysis, multimedia reportage and artistic display, involving some thirty artists in an attempt to expose the conditions of exploitation, expropriation and impoverishment in an Argentinean province. The participants, who had drawn their conclusions from the most advanced theoretical positions and technical experiments of the time, chose to break with the existing institutions in the hope of infiltrating the national information system and contributing directly to the political struggle against the Onganía dictatorship. *Tucumán Arde* is increasingly recognized as a genealogical departure point for the kinds of media activism practiced today.[3] But can we not also read Carnevale's enclosure piece as an allegory of the way that social classes are transformed under conditions of urgency?

In the late nineties, the politically involved sectors of the overdeveloped countries—the NGOs, the charities, the unionists, the communists and ecologists—were the people inside the glass bubble of consensus, or "civil-society dialogue." It was the direct actionists who shattered the window.

We know that the cycle of massive demonstrations that began in the years 1999–2001 was no miracle. The impetus had come from the South, primarily from social movements in Latin America and India. The global justice campaigns, inspired by South African efforts to force debt cancellation, had built a tremendous following. Critique of neoliberalism had become a national issue in both France and Canada. The labor movements of the overdeveloped countries were ripe for radicalization. And the Zapatistas offered a new model of political confrontation, combining powerful symbolic actions with national and international networks of support. But political forces must be set into motion, passions have to catch flame. In the cities of Western Europe and North America, where the postmodern waning of affect appeared to be complete, it was the urban cultures of resistance that struck the match. Reclaim the Streets in Great Britain, the Tute Bianche in Italy, the Direct Action Network of the Pacific Northwest United States—these were the catalysts that transformed a diffuse aspiration of isolated civil-society groups into a movement, able to take to the streets and reach beyond the specific demands of each dissenting group.

A political generation is forged, not by determinants of age, but by choices of involvement and experiences of confrontation. How are such choices made? The invitation to illegal protest that sparked the current cycle of anticapitalist mobilizations aimed to draw out the participation of social categories, particularly youth, who could no longer be lured into involvement by identity issues, parties or unions. But it also sought to bring more traditional formations into heightened conflict. The success of the Direct Action Network in Seattle, at the WTO meeting in November 1999, was to use civil-disobedience techniques to immobilize traffic in a key sector of the city, focusing police repression and in this way creating a magnetic attractor for union members exiting from their consensually managed events—but also for local inhabitants, ecologists, Third World delegations, anarchists and many others. Through that intervention a five-day urban uprising was unleashed. In a less disciplined yet equally potent way, the Reclaim the Streets carnivals offered a tantalizing cocktail of transgressive pleasure, informed political protest and direct confrontation, which radicalized the participants by exposing the structural violence of contemporary social relations. But the Tute Bianche of Italy ("White Overalls") developed the most explicit strategy. The white overall, which could be donned by anyone, signified the permeability of a movement that was not ideological in the disciplinary sense. The use of quite ridiculous-looking protective padding created a theatrics of humor and self-derision, while allowing police brutality to be captured on video as a kind of comic spectacle. Most importantly, the duration of this movement was limited in advance by the prediction of its self-dissolution into all the colors. The release from a paralyzing consensus became constitutive of the movement.

It would be misleading to claim that the direct actionists played the role of a vanguard artist, leading a naive public into an experiential trap where every participant would be forced to draw fresh conclusions. The self-transformation of society is more complicated, more multiple, than Carnevale's enclosure piece can suggest. Yet the imprint of artistic experimentation on the current political generation is undeniable. The most obvious contribution of the visual arts to the anticapitalist movements is the merger of community-oriented video with the distribution system offered by Internet, giving rise to innumerable non-normalized media projects that combine documentary information and expressive politics, in the lineage of *Tucumán Arde*. These projects carry out a specular combat with broadcast TV—that is, with the spectacle society—and in that way, they at least partially fulfill the political aspirations of the early videomakers. Another, more subtle thread is the proliferation of mail art, first through 'zine culture and desktop publishing, then through the net, culminating in the mid-nineties in the widespread circulation of subversive texts and media pranks under multiple names like Monty Cantsin or Luther Blissett. Multiple names bring the refusal of copyright and intellectual property to the very center of ego-dominated subjectivity, in an attempt to dissolve the proprietary function of the signature which has always served as the barrier between contemplative, individualistic art and collective, interactive forms of expression. Yet another artistic contribution to the movements is performance culture, with its emphasis on the embodiment of the political, played out in its inseparability from the sexual, ritual, generational, ethnic, and psychodramatic dimensions of human experience. One could be tempted to conceive the entire *dispositif* of the carnivalesque demonstration as an extension of performance to the streets. But if we stopped there we would miss the deepest commonality between experimental art and the activism. This is the notion of process, as a value in and of itself.

In the now-canonical "anti-form" definitions of the sixties, process designates the temporal dimension of materials, their transformation in time, as initiated or continuously effected by the activity of the artist. But there is another definition, whose roots lie in the chance philosophy of John Cage, in the relation of prop and performance sought by Fluxus, in the interplay of score and interpretation developed in concrete poetry and vanguard dance, in the orchestrated chaos of the happenings, the improvisational work of the Living Theater or the insurgency of Provo and Situationist interventions. In these approaches, process can be defined as the generative matrix constituted by the meeting of catalytic artifacts, more-or-less conscious group interactions, and the dimension of singular chance inherent to the event. This artistic understanding of the way that "social material" can proactively transform itself over time was enriched by the movements of anti-psychiatry and schizoanalysis, which extended the domain of what could be accepted as self-expression, and attempted to reshape institutional structures to accommodate the multiplication of subjective forms. The micropolitics of a host of liberation movements of the seventies, including the women's movements in particular, but also the local constellations of Italian Autonomia, made group processes of self-understanding and decision-making into one of the ways that adherence to a political project is developed and sustained over time. The difference of the last ten or fifteen years is that the proliferation of expressive practices in everyday life—inseparable from the rise of intellectual and affective labor[4]—has brought the specifically artistic definition of social process back to the forefront, not within the art world but in the more open and uncontrollable space of the urban event.

The fundamental relation between post-vanguard art and contemporary social movements is here, in this resurgence of expressive and interactive process which has helped forge a political generation. What it gives us to understand is that an entire current of experimentalism has migrated outside the realm of art as defined by the signature-work. But this realization is only the departure point for a series of questions, concerning the political postures that have developed as a necessary exodus from the immobilizing transparency of the mediated democracies. The questions are these: Why was the mix of carnival and direct action so important to the protagonism of civil society? How has the situation changed since September 11? What will happen to the new political generation that emerged just before the authoritarian turn? And what roles can artists play in that generation's development?

CIVIL SOCIETY IN A HALL OF MIRRORS

I've suggested that art can be compared to activism through the metaphor of an intervention on "social material." The idea might sound scandalous; yet just such a process lies behind the emergence of what we now recognize as global civil society. In the late seventies and early eighties, Eastern European writers like Adam Michnik, Václav Havel and Gyorgy Konrad used a combination of literary expression and political critique to redefine the classical concept of national civil society, and in this way, to precipitate a change in collective consciousness. No longer would civil society be simply understood as the pacifying rule of law within the boundaries of a sovereign territory; nor just as the right of citizens to engage in critical discourse. Instead it would designate the need to create an everyday space of civic engagement that effectively secedes from the totalitarian state. For Konrad, civil society was an *anti-politics*. As he wrote in 1982, "Anti-politics is the emergence of forums that can be appealed to against political power; it is a counter-power that cannot take power and does not wish to."[5] The Czech dissidents spoke of a *parallel polis*, which, as Václav Benda explained, "does not compete for power. Its aim is not to replace the power of another kind, but rather under this power—or beside it—to create a structure that represents other laws and in which the voice of the ruling power is heard only as an insignificant echo from a world that is organized in an entirely different way."[6] Because the Soviet and American blocs were widely perceived as two sides of the same coin—both threatening nuclear violence on a scale that dwarfed the traditional, nationally bounded space of civility—it was immediately considered necessary to extend the rightful space of anti-politics to global dimensions. Konrad maintained that the "existence of a world forum favors the emergence of the eccentric, those who stand out." And he continued: "The international alliance of dissenters and avant-gardists takes under its wing those few people who, in their various ways, think their thoughts through to the end."[7]

Similar ideas developed in South America, in the face of the dictatorships. The aim was to open up a myriad of divergent and ultimately uncontrollable micropolitical spaces, in order to succeed where the guerrilla struggles had failed.[8] This conception of divergent spaces remains an important legacy for anti-systemic movements, as witnessed by the Zapatista autonomous zones, the Social Forums, John Holloway's call to change the world without taking power, or Paolo Virno's notion of a non-state public sphere. But there has been a critical change since the eighties. No one today can ignore the deeply ambiguous role that civil society would play after 1989—especially since Michnik, Havel and Konrad have all supported the invasion of Iraq.[9] The more recent attempts to intervene on social material have all had to respond to the bewildering metamorphosis of civil society after the collapse of the Soviet Union.

The integration of a diluted concept of civil society to the reality of capitalist globalization was a consequence of the ideological vacuum left by 1989. In the absence of any coordinated oppositional force, every critique could be considered at worst harmless, and at best, profitable. The exploitation of humanitarian NGOs by the neoliberal state is there to prove it—along with the corporate patronage of critical art. Yet the nineties were also a time of opening. Air transportation, global communications and international coordination were now accessible even to informal groups. The structures of governance became more transnational but more transparent too, permeable to the public, permeated by the media, constantly overseen by innumerable observers. The paradox of civil society in the years of Clinton, Blair, Jospin and Schroeder was to sit on all kinds of official panels, to be aired on all kinds of channels and to be allowed to debate about everything, except the basic values that orient the post-'89 world-system.

Such was the Western *glasnost*. The hidden aims of public relations and private sponsorship, the realpolitik of elected office and international commissions, and the increasing insistence of the news media on the rules of a world marketplace in which they themselves are major players, all gave civil-society figures the uncanny sensation of moving in a hall of mirrors. As though transparency in the mediated democracies could only be found in a camera lens, whose function is to select and frame, even before the image is recorded, edited, repurposed and broadcast as the opposite of whatever was initially intended. In the late nineties, Havel's warning in his famous 1978 essay on "The Power of the Powerless" was timelier than ever, despite or even because of the presidential office occupied by its author: "It would appear that traditional parliamentary democracies can offer no fundamental opposition to the automatism of technological civilization and the industrial-consumer society, for they too are being dragged helplessly along by it. People are manipulated in ways that are infinitely more subtle and refined than the brutal methods used in the post-totalitarian societies."[10]

By the end of Clinton's imperial mandate, the need for direct action became obvious—at least to those on the fringes. Because they did not claim to be civil anymore, deliberate gestures of disobedience could break the distorting mirror and reclaim the density and opacity of an oppositional position. Only this kind of confrontation could make activists from the South take the Northern protests seriously. But the carnivalesque dimension, the artistic treatment of information and the experimentation with social process are not just window dressing for a protestor's brick. These are the ways that participants have found to reinvent the anti-political space of everyday experience, despite full-spectrum attempts at commercial, cultural, governmental and ideological mediation.

It's often said that September 11 put an end to the effectiveness of direct action protests, by delegitimating anything that could be assimilated to terrorism and authorizing massive deployment of the police. That's true, and the strategy had already been sketched out in Genoa. But the consequences of September 11 on the US government have had the long-term effect of demonstrating that the fusion of the state with a corporate oligarchy can produce a repressive apparatus that stretches its electronic fingers into every aspect of daily life. We are witnessing the onset of a social pathology, comparable in scale if not in nature to the Cold War. And only idealists could believe that the European bloc is not producing its own variations on this pathology, for instance in the treatment of immigrant workers and the nationalist rhetoric surrounding the presence of so-called foreigners, or in the establishment of detainment camps inside and outside the EU borders.[11] But to oppose the security panic and the reality of institutional racism that underlies it would mean refusing the false transparencies, escaping the co-optation machinery of parliamentary democracy itself. This is why in the very moment of their rise to visibility and to more complex forms of organization, dissenting social movements have begun to experiment once again with new forms of anti-politics, marked by the pragmatics of defection and exit, but also by the more intangible, almost mythical theme of exodus.

REDISAPPEARING

A strange and quite funny anecdote from the European Social Forum in Florence, in November 2002, can help make the point. Faced with an overload of slogans like "Stop this Bloody War" and "Another World Is Possible"—which is like a marriage of Trotskyist populism and civil-society naiveté—members of the Euraction Hub network decided to intervene. They used the materials at hand. An activist in an outlandish blue wig was installed on the roof of a van outfitted with projecting pink wings; this emissary from the outside advanced within a compact crowd toward the Fortezza da Basso, a medieval castle where the main events were being held for paying admission. Vanquishing the objections of the security team, the procession entered the Forum to have a dance party right next to the circus tent where SWP Trots were bellowing out slogans from 1917. As the perimeter of the castle was crossed, the activists raised a banner that read: "Stop the World, Another War Is Possible."

The satire of consensus was perfect—and so was the call for massive direct action that would paralyze entire cities. The banner in the gateway expressed the widespread desire for something more effective than the global antiwar demonstrations of February 15, 2003, which were in fact proposed at the ESF meeting in Florence. Along with this idea of mass defection from the militarized societies, it asserted the possibility of a wholly *other war*: a subversion that could dissolve normalized behaviors and established hierarchies.[12] The networked activists had not forgotten that Deleuze and Guattari conceived their nomadic war machine as a potential of expressive and epistemological variance that could operate within every institution, and even at the heart of the military-industrial complexes. They had not forgotten, because the development of the Internet over more than thirty years has proved this kind of subversion to be a practical reality. Such struggles necessarily take place within the capture-devices that seek to neutralize them: thus the entry of the activists into the castle, as a way to pursue the exit from politics-as-usual that had launched the entire social forum movement in the first place. Without a constant resurgence of the radicalizing process, grassroots mobilization can be halted by the very organizations and figureheads it needs in order to expand its field of transformation. But this is what has been learned since the early demands for the representation of civil society. The destinies of the current political generation depend crucially on maintaining the possibilities both of large-scale organized confrontation, and of direct, micropolitical participation in the processes of self-government.[13]

These understandings appear clearly in the new mobilizations around precarious labor, articulated among others by the French part-time cinema and theater workers and the EuroMayday paraders in Milan and Barcelona.[14] These confrontational movements, which make a great use of street performance and artistic invention but also of very specific juridical and sociological knowledge, can be seen as attempts to infiltrate, destabilize and reconfigure the social state. Not only is a new kind of labor to be considered—part-time or interim workers—but also a new set of claims, which mix wage and social insurance issues with the demand for more free time and better opportunities to use it. The treatment of casual labor becomes a question of human ecology. Thus what is ostensibly a workers' movement builds constitutive links to struggles over unemployment, education, environmental conditions, real-estate speculation and the commodification of culture. The massive presence of migrants in the circuits of precarious labor brings in concrete North-South issues of unequal exchange as well, and thereby lends these campaigns at least the potential to act with the full political composition that first appeared in Seattle and Genoa. In this way, unionizing strategies can remain part of a larger struggle, which requires a multiperspectival awareness of its protagonists. The goal is to transform the state, but without becoming it—that is, without being subjected by its market imperatives and bureaucratic categories. Only in this way can the horizons of social change remain open enough to embrace the world.

Artists and media activists participate directly in these movements and at the same time symbolize them, by condensing their experience of the radicalizing process into expressive works. The distribution of these works, through alternative circuits and then gradually through broader institutional formats, is a way to give complexity and consistency to the affects of rebellion and refusal. But the familiar limits have not vanished. The basic functions of selection and framing, editing and repurposing, are performed in perfect transparency by the gallery-magazine-museum system. As the demand for an activist aesthetic rises, the selection will almost inevitably come to focus on dramatized images of insurgency, associated with a truncated genealogy of theoretical concepts from the late sixties and early seventies. In other words, the presentations will slice out a few visual and conceptual elements from a longer, broader and more complex history, leaving the viewer untroubled by any kind of processual passion. A new institutional critique might then arise, denouncing the failure of museums to adequately inform the public. But in reality, it is the inherent failure of representation, both in the visual and the political sense, that continually leads activist-artists to abandon their works and their familiar skills, and to dissolve once again into the intersubjective processes of society's self-transformation.

This moment of dissolution is where one could locate exodus, not as a concept, but as a power or a myth of resistance. On the one hand, exodus is a pragmatic response to the society of control, in which any widespread political opposition becomes an object of exacting analysis for those who can afford to invest major resources in the identification, segmentation and manipulation of what we naively call the public. In the face of these strategies, exodus is a power of willful metamorphosis: the capacity for a movement to appear, to intervene and to disappear again, before changing names and recommencing the same struggle in a different way. And this too is a process that artists can symbolize, by performing the self-overcoming of art once again—at the risk of dissolving their proper names, their trademarks and their careers. But the very statement of this tactical necessity of disappearance raises a deep anxiety, which must be familiar to all old revolutionaries, about the possible continuity of resistant culture, or the constitution over time of something like an anti-systemic movement. In this regard, exodus seems to designate an existential reserve, that psychic space where fragments of artistic, poetic and musical refrains are inseparable from the wellsprings of action, but expressible only as a kind of myth.[15] To touch this intangible space is the ultimate intervention on social material—something no individual can do, because it is only achieved through a collective experience, by a multiplicity that has no authority, no signature.

Exodus is an expression of process politics. It points beyond the distorting mediations and structural inequalities of capitalism toward a strange sort of promised land for the profane, which is the immediacy of the everyday, the direct experience of cooperation with others. The carnival that sometimes breaks out in the midst of concerted political action is a way to celebrate the occasional reality of this powerful and persistent myth.

Notes

1 F. Guattari, "The Left as a Processual Passion," in G. Genosko, ed., *The Guattari Reader* (London: Blackwell, 1996), p. 260.
2 G. Carnevale, catalogue text, "Ciclo de Arte Experimental," in Ana Longoni and Mariano Mestman, *Del Di Tella a "Tucumán Arde"* (Buenos Aires: El Cielo Por Asalto, 2000), p. 122.
3 Cf. M. Carmen Ramírez, "Thriving on Adversity: Conceptualism in Latin America, 1960-1980," in *Global Conceptualism: Points of Origin, 1950s-1980s*, catalogue, Queens Museum of Art, 1999, pp. 66-67;as well as M.T. Gramuglio and N. Rosa, "Tucumán Burns," in *Conceptual Art: A Critical Anthology*, eds. A. Alberro and B. Stimson (Cambridge, Mass.: MIT Press, 1999), pp. 76-79.
4 For the relation between labor and expressive politics, see Paolo Virno, "Virtuosity and Revolution: the Political Theory of Exodus," in M. Hardt and P. Virno, eds., *Radical Thought in Italy* (Minneapolis: University of Minnesota Press, 1996), available at: www.makeworlds.org/book/view/34.
5 G. Konrad, *Anti-Politics: An Essay* (New York: Harcourt, Brace, Jovanovich, 1984), p. 231.
6 V. Benda, quoted in Mary Kaldor, *Global Civil Society* (London: Polity, 2003), p. 56.

7 G. Konrad, *Anti-Politics: An Essay*, op. cit., p. 211.
8 For the Brazilian situation in the early eighties, see Félix Guattari and Suely Rolnik, *Cartography of Desire: Schizoanalysis in Brazil* (forthcoming from MIT/Semiotexte).
9 Michnik justified himself and his two peers in an article entitled "We, the Traitors," published in his own newspaper, *Gazeta Wyborzca*, Warsaw, March 28, 2003, available in English at: www.worldpress.org/Europe/1086.cfm.
10 V. Havel, "The Power of the Powerless," in J. Keane, ed., *The Power of the Powerless* (London: Hutchinson, 1985), p. 91.
11 Cf. I. Saint-Saëns, "Des camps en Europe aux camps de l'Europe," in *Multitudes* 19, Paris, December 2004.
12 For the subversive philosophy of this slogan, see the Spanish-language publication "sic": http://sindominio.net/ofic2004/publicaciones/sic/indice0.html.
13 For an understanding of the way this contradiction is being discussed within the Social Forum movement, see the issue of the web-journal *ephemera* on "The Organisation and Politics of Social Forums," downloadable at http://www.ephemeraweb.org/journal/5-2/5-2ephemera-may05.pdf.
14 Cf. www.cip-idf.org and www.euromayday.org.
15 Cf. F. Guattari, *Chaosmosis: An ethico-aesthetic paradigm* (Bloomington: Indiana University Press, 1995), esp. pp. 19–20, 60–61.

More Titles in Politics & Culture from Autonomedia

Subverting the Present, Imagining the Future
INSURRECTION, MOVEMENT, COMMONS
Werner Bonefeld, editor

To subvert is to bring to the fore what is hidden beneath the forms of bourgeois respectability – a respectability in which every human contents has its price. To subvert is to imagine the communist individual in revolt against any system – economic, political, cultural or religious – where humanity is no more than an object to be manipulated, exploited, and dominated. This volume examines the social-historical constitution of capitalism and its dynamic, analyses the contemporary means of subversion-in-movement, and assesses the trajectory of struggles in the Americas, from Argentina to Mexico, from Bolivia to the United States of America. Authors include the Midnight Notes Collective, Massimo De Angelis, Werner Bonefeld, Paul Zarembka, Maria-rosa Dalla Costa, the Leeds May Day Group, Harry Cleaver, Nick Dyer-Witheford, Stevphen Shukaitis, Ana Dinerstein, George Caffentzis, Conrad Herold, Patrick Cuninghame, and Sergio Tischler.
ISBN: 978-1-57027-184-7   320 pages   6"x9"

Marching Plague
GERM WARFARE AND GLOBAL PUBLIC HEALTH
Critical Art Ensemble

Our sixth Critical Art Ensemble title offers a radical reframing of the rhetoric surrounding germ warfare. After refuting the idea that massive biological attack is a probable future occurrence, the book goes on to argue that biological weapons programs primarily serve the economic interests of the military-security complex, squandering resources needed to fight the massive loss of life each year from emerging infectious diseases. The book also includes two appendices examining the case of the U.S. Justice Department against Steve Kurtz, for which the original manuscript of the book was seized in the state's investigation.
ISBN: 1-57027-178-X   192 pages   4½"x7"

Gynocide
HYSTERRECTOMY, CAPITALIST PATRIARCHY & MEDICAL ABUSE OF WOMEN
Mariarosa Dalla Costa, editor

These essays and accompanying glossaries and testimonials — focused on hysterrectomy — examine the historical, legal, ethical, psychological amd medical aspects of deeply sexist practices in defining and treating issues of contemporary women's health. Contributors draw on the important theoretical perspectives developed in recent years by radical Italian feminism, revealing the complicity of widespread assumptions about the structures and roles of gender, the nuclear family, educational practices, and the state.   ISBN: 978-1-57027-176-2   160 pages   6"x9"

Escape From the 19th Century
ESSAYS ON MARX, FOURIER, PROUDHON AND NIETZSCHE
Peter Lamborn Wilson

Did the nineteenth century ever come to an end? Was the twentieth century just a re-run? If to know "History" as tragedy is to escape its repetition as farce, then perhaps we need to look more deeply at this Past that won't stop haunting us. Two illuminated madmen—Charles Fourier and Friedrich Nietzsche—and two too-sane geniuses—J.-P. Proudhon and Karl Marx—are enlisted in the break-out plan. The shape of this plan is then suggested in a final essay showing how old "rights and customs" of paleolithic reciprocity and eqalitarian spirituality have made innumerable re-entries into History.   ISBN: 1-57027-073-2 1998 206pp. 6"x9" $14.95

MORE TITLES IN POLITICS & CULTURE FROM AUTONOMEDIA

The Art of Free Cooperation
Geert Lovink & Trebor Scholz, eds.

Inspired by the collaborative models of non-proprietary "open source" software, new German writer Christoph Spehr, Howard Rheingold, Brian Holmes and the editors critique both the received capitalist and socialist methods of social integration, and elaborate a practical vision for a third alternative, one that promises to surmount the problems of inequality on the one hand and the lack of individual freedoms on the other. Part performative intervention, part radical polemic and activist manual, *The Art of Free Cooperation* includes a DVD with additional interviews and performance highlights with Spehr and others.   ISBN 978-1-57027-177-9   224 pages + DVD   6"x9"

Provo
AMSTERDAM'S ANARCHIST REVOLT
Richard Kempton

This is the first book-length English-language study of Holland's legendary insurrectional movement. In an introduction and eight chapters, Richard Kempton narrates the rise and fall of Provo from early Dutch "Happenings" staged in 1962 through to the so-called "Death of Provo" in 1967, including Robert Jasper Grootveld's anarchist anti-cancer campaigns, the riots against Princess Beatrix's marriage to an ex-Nazi, and the famous White Bicycle program. Then, in seven appendices, he comments on parallel contemporary and near-contemporary movements, including Dada and Situationism; studies Amsterdam's previous anarchist traditions; chronicles the spread of Provo through the Netherlands and the development of the Kabouter (Gnome) party; and offers an existentialist critique of Provo and other anarchist movements of the '60s. This unique book is based on extensive primary research and includes a selective bibliography of the Dutch-language sources.   ISBN: 978-1-57027-181-6   256 pages   6"x9"

Black Fez Manifesto, Etc.
Hakim Bey

New poetic rants and prose poems from the pseudonymous author of *TAZ* and *Millennium*, among many other influential, incendiary texts. "BLACK FEZ is the emblem of our intransigent disgust with the lukewarm necromantic vacuum of dephlogisticated corpse breath that passes nowadays for Empire and organic death."   ISBN: 978-1-57027-187-8   128 pages   6"x9"

The Work of Love
UNPAID HOUSEWORK, POVERTY & SEXUAL VIOLENCE AT THE DAWN OF THE 21ST CENTURY
Giovanna Franca Dalla Costa

This text poses, at the center of its analysis, the relationship which exists between physical (and specifically sexual) violence against women, and the role of women in performing housework, to which they remain primarily assigned in the global capitalist division of labor (and which seeks to define all of their existence).   ISBN: 978-1-57027-132-8   160 pages   6"x9"

This World We Must Leave and Other Essays
Jacques Camatte

Post-Marxist essays coming out of the spirit of '68 France, but from a less familiar angle. Neither a Parisian poststructuralist academic nor a situationist, Camatte comes from an ultraleft Franco-Italian communist background, and takes Marx in a more ecological and anarchistic direction.
ISBN: 1-57027-020-1   256pp.   4½"x7"

More Titles in Politics & Culture from Autonomedia

Forbidden Sacraments
THE SURVIVAL OF SHAMANISM IN WESTERN CIVILIZATION
Donald P. Dulchinos

The indigenous practice of shamanism has been under siege for as long as Western European societies have practiced colonialism and Christian missionary work. Only very recently has there been a backlash condemning the cultural chauvinism that labels indigenous shamanism "primitive." Increasingly, shaman-centered cultures are respected for values of community, environmental consciousness, and first-hand spiritual experience. What is not widely known is that Western civilization itself, beneath layers of Christianity and industrialism, stands upon its own shamanic foundation. ISBN: 978-1-57027-111-3   192 pages   6"x9"

Dreamer of the Day
FRANCIS PARKER YOCKEY AND THE POSTWAR FASCIST INTERNATIONAL
Kevin Coogan

Francis Parker Yockey, a lawyer and former war-crimes prosecutor, was one of the most enigmatic figures inside the far right in both Europe and America. While he is best known today for his book *Imperium*, a huge tome often described as a *Mein Kampf* for modern-day neo-Nazis, his life remains a mystery. Pursued by the U.S. Government for almost a decade, Yockey was arrested by the FBI in 1960. Shortly after his capture, he was found dead in his jail cell. An autopsy showed that the 43-year old mystery man had swallowed a cyanide capsule. Yockey's story takes us into the heart of the postwar Fascist International, a shadow Reich composed of spies, conspirators, and occultists.
ISBN: 1-57027-039-2 648pp. 6"x9"

Blue-Eyed Devil
A ROAD ODYSSEY THROUGH ISLAMIC AMERICA
Michael Muhammed Knight

In his quest for an indigenous "American Islam," Michael Muhammad Knight embarked on a series of interstate odysseys. Traveling 20,000 miles by Greyhound in sixty days, he squatted in run-down mosques, pursued Muslim romance, was detained at the U.S.-Canadian border with a trunkload of Shi'a literature, crashed Islamic Society of North America conventions, stink-palmed Cat Stevens, limped across Chicago to find the grave of Noble Drew Ali, and hunted down the truth of the Nation of Islam mystery-man, W.D. Fard — filling dozens of notebooks along the way. In the course of his adventures Knight sorted out his own relationship to Islam as he journeys from punk provocateur to a recognized voice in the community, and watches first-hand the collapse of a liberal Islamic dream, the Progressive Muslim Union. Taking a unique perspective on Islam's intersection with race, gender, and Americanization, *Blue-Eyed Devil* offers a brutally honest but ultimately compassionate look at the marginal underground of Islamic America.
ISBN: 978-1-57027-179-3   224 pages   6"x9"

Toward Secession
156 MORE POLITICAL ESSAYS
Richard Kostelanetz

The impossibly prolific anarchist and libertarian cultural critic offers a rich second volume of collected political essays, ranging from the title effort to further assaults on power and privilege in a vast array of topics, including Bush, 9/11, the Middle East, terrorism, pedophilia, Noam Chomsky, Jane Jacobs, Alexander Cockburn, Christopher Hitchens, Norman O. Brown, Ayn Rand, Frank Zappa, George Orwell, Karl Hess, and Fidel Castro.
ISBN: 978-1-57027-195-3   342 pages   6"x9"

MORE TITLES IN POLITICS & CULTURE FROM AUTONOMEDIA

Caliban and the Witch
WOMEN, THE BODY, & PRIMITIVE ACCUMULATION
Silvia Federici

Caliban and the Witch is a history of the body in the transition to capitalism. Moving from the peasant revolts of the late Middle Ages to the witch hunts and the rise of mechanical philosophy, Federici investigates the capitalist rationalization of social reproduction. She shows how the struggle against the rebel body and the conflict between body and mind are essential conditions for the development of labor power and self-ownership, two central principles of modern social organization.
ISBN: 1-57027-059-7   2004   288pp.   6"x9" $15.95

Akiba
A GNOSTIC NOVEL
p.m.

In the 1980s, p.m.'s book *bolo'bolo* became an indispensable guide to new autonomous projects, a manual for "applied utopias"on a human scale, stressing cultural diversity, freedom of movement, ecological sustainability, and a relaxed attitude towards work — themes which remain essential in his new novel. Akiba combines the age-old schemes of millennial and modern utopias with recent research in ecology, quantum physics and computing, the mathematics of the Big Bang, Peak Oil theories, and the work of Roger Penrose, J. R. Searle, and others.
ISBN: 978-1-57027-176-2   274 pages   6"x9"

Ethereal Shadows
COMMUNICATIONS AND POWER IN CONTEMPORARY ITALY
Franco "Bifo" Berardi and Marco Jacquemet

Focusing on the recent Italian "videocracy," this book documents the emergence of the first Italian media mogul, Silvio Berlusconi, and his rise to and recent fall from political power. It also explores Italian media activism through three case studies: a discussion of the first autonomous free radio station, Radio Alice (which broadcasted in Bologna between 1977 and 1979); a review of Italian Internet activism focusing on a political site, Rekombinant.org (created in 2000); and finally a chronicle of the emergence in 2002 of OrfeoTV, the first Italian example of an illegal micro-TV station.   ISBN: 978-1-57027-188-5   224 pages   6"x9"

Anarchitexts
VOICES FROM THE GLOBAL DIGITAL UNDERGROUND
Joanne Richardson, editor

Radical essays from the global underground on art, technology, autonomous culture and the politics of the future. Writers and artists from Russia, Romania, India, Yugoslavia, Hungary, Italy, Germany, Mexico, Slovenia, Poland, Austria, England, Croatia, Japan, Latvia, Bulgaria, the Netherlands, Canada, France, Australia, Spain and the US.   ISBN: 1-57027-146-1   368 pages, 6"x9"

Sound Generation
Alexis Bhagat & Greg Gangemi, eds.

Sound Generation is a polyvocal mashup of innovative voices from the world of sound art, mixed by the editors to reveal lines of thought on the politics of audio. Contributors include Gregory Whitehead, Annea Lockwood, Grey Filastine, Maryanne Amacher, Ken Montgomery, Pamela Z, and Hildegard Westerkamp.   ISBN: 978-1-57027-183-0   256 pages   7½x7½"

Revolutionary Writing
COMMON SENSE ESSAYS IN POST-POLITICAL POLITICS
Werner Bonefeld, editor
After a century of failed attempts to bring about radical social change, the concept of revolution is itself in crisis. What does anti-capitalism in its contemporary form of anti-globalization mean if it is not a practical critique of capitalism, and what does it wish to achieve if its anti-capitalism fails to espouse the revolutionary project of human emancipation? The misery of our time demands that we, once again, dream revolution... that is, orient our theoretical and practical activities on the ideal of the society of the free and equal. ISBN: 1-57027-133-X 256pp. 6"x9"

TAZ
THE TEMPORARY AUTONOMOUS ZONE, ONTOLOGICAL ANARCHISM, POETIC TERRORISM
Hakim Bey
The underground cult bestseller! Essays redefining the psychogeographical nooks of autonomy. Recipes for poetic terror, anarcho-black magic, post-situ psychotropic surgery, denunciations of spiritual addictions to vapid infotainment cults—this is the bastard classic, the watermark impressed upon our minds. Where conscience informs praxis, and action infects consciousness, *T.A.Z.* continues to worm its way into above-ground culture. Second edition, with a new introductory essay by the author and additional appendical materials. ISBN: 1-57027-151-8 160pp. 4½"x7"

Surrealist Subversions
RANTS, WRITINGS & IMAGES FROM THE SURREALIST MOVEMENT IN THE U.S
Ron Sakolsky, editor
From its auspicious beginnings in the summer of 1966 to the present, the Chicago Surrealist Group — and the Surrealist Movement in the United States, which grew out of it — has brightly illuminated the pathways of absolute divergence that define the intrinsically anarchist trajectory of the surrealist adventure. Drawing on the full range of U.S. surrealist publications and communiques from the front lines of the battle against miserabilism, this volume contains over 200 texts (many appearing here for the first time) by more than 50 participants, in the most comprehensive, diverse and lavishly illustrated compilation of American surrealist writings ever assembled. ISBN: 1-57027-122-4 750pp. 6"x9"

Marx Beyond Marx
LESSONS ON THE GRÜNDRISSE
Antonio Negri
A key figure in the Italian "Autonomia" Movement reads Marx's Gründrisse, developing the critical and controversial theoretical apparatus that informs the "zero-work" strategy and other elements so crucial to this new and "heretical" tendency in Marxist theory. A challenge to both capitalist and socialist apologists for waged slavery. ISBN: 0-936756-25-X 256pp. 6"x9"

I Am Not A Man, I Am Dynamite!
FRIEDRICH NIETZSCHE AND THE ANARCHIST TRADITION
John Moore, editor
Though Nietzsche never called himself an anarchist, his philosophy and writing have provided inspiration and instruction for many of the 20th century's primary anarchist voices. Examines various dimensions of Nietzsche's thought among historical and contemporary anarchist thinkers, hammering out a philosophical iconoclasm much overlooked in historical surveys.
ISBN: 1-57027-121-6 192pp. 6"x9"